BERLITZ®

ROME

- A ☑ in the text denotes a highly recommended sight
- A complete A–Z of practical information starts on p.113
- Extensive mapping on cover flaps

Printed in Switzerland by Weber SA, Bienne.

2nd edition (1994/1995)

Although we make every effort to ensure the accuracy of the information in this guide, changes do occur. If you have any new information, suggestions or corrections to contribute, we would like to hear from you. Please write to Berlitz Publishing at the above address.

Text:	Jason Best
Editors:	Nicola Gadsby, Sarah Hudson
Photography:	Jon Davison, except pp.7, 31, 86, 103 Jason Best
Layout:	Suzanna Boyle
Cartography:	🅕 Falk-Verlag, Hamburg
Thanks to:	the staff of the Rome Tourist Board, Amanda Cruise and Samantha Velluti.

Cover photograph: Trevi Fountain, © The Telegraph Colour Library

CONTENTS

Rome and the Romans

In the 27 centuries of its existence, Rome has seen empires rise and fall, popes and caesars come and go, and artistic movements flourish and fade. Throughout all the different eras, however, there has been one strong thread of continuity: the Eternal City has always been changing.

Furthermore, Rome doesn't stand still today. As a modern European capital, it just can't afford to rest on its laurels. It must play the part of an up-to-date political and business city while simultaneously attempting to preserve its enormous cultural inheritance.

The wealth of Rome's patrimony makes most other cities look like paupers. For a start, there are its great ancient remains: the Pantheon, still inspiring awe after almost 2,000 years; the terrible majesty of the Colosseum; the poignant ruins of the Roman Forum. Then there is the cool beauty of the early Christian basilicas and the heritage of medieval Rome, complete with all its glorious mosaics and tranquil cloisters.

The Renaissance is reflected in elegant churches, graceful palaces and the renowned genius of painters Raphael and Michelangelo. Finally, as if that wasn't enough, the baroque era offers dynamic architecture, theatrical piazzas and a host of flamboyant fountains.

Visitors will quite likely be bowled over by this panoply of treasures, but today's Romans take them in their stride. They're accustomed to conducting their lives against this awesome backdrop, drinking tap water from an aqueduct which was probably constructed by a Roman consul and restored by a Renaissance pope.

Perhaps they take Rome too much for granted. It's refreshing that the city is not treated as an open-air museum, but less cheering that many real museums remain closed for years on end while bureaucrats wrangle over renovation costs and staffing levels. Medieval **5**

Romans burned marble statues to obtain lime; modern Romans' love affair with the internal combustion engine does almost as much damage today. During the last few decades, exhaust fumes and traffic vibrations have had a catastrophic impact on monuments.

*T*he traffic *polizia are a familiar sight – but Rome is not the best place for out-of-town drivers.*

Some things are improving, however. Traffic has been banned from large areas of the historic centre, church façades have been given face-lifts, and scaffolding has been removed from ancient columns and triumphal arches.

Today the magnificent equestrian bronze statue of Emperor Marcus Aurelius, who spent the 1980s undergoing restoration, is now firmly back on the Campidoglio, although it's behind protective glass. In addition, billions of lire are now being spent on *Roma Capitale*, a massive programme of public works designed to enhance the status of the city.

Progress is painfully slow, meanwhile. The ancient Romans rushed out to conquer an empire and make their city the *caput mundi* – 'capital of the world'. Their descendants have unfortunately not been quite as quick off the mark. Since becoming the capital of the newly united Italy in 1870, Rome's record as the nation's seat of government has been somewhat marked by inefficiency and inertia.

Don't be deceived by the hurtling traffic or the bustling activity you witness in markets and on the streets; the pace of life in Rome is really rather leisurely. Geographically as well as psychologically, the city is closer to the laid-back south than the go-ahead north of Italy.

Observe how, in time-honoured fashion, the entire city comes to a complete standstill during the early afternoon. Between 1 and 2pm shops, businesses and market stalls close and everyone goes home for lunch. Some then take a siesta,

Just one of the symbols of Rome, the mighty St Peter's Basilica has awe-inspiring dimensions.

while others, particularly those state employees whose official working day finishes at 2pm, go off to the undeclared second jobs that make Italy's black economy the biggest in Europe.

L'orario Americano, as the Italians call the 9-to-5 working day, has found very few admirers in Rome.

7

*D*aily life in Rome – people-watching from a café on the historic Piazza Navona or a ride on a city tram along the Via Aventino.

As for visitors, don't fret over whether or not to follow the famous maxim of 'When in Rome ...' – the rhythms of the Roman day will oblige you to do as the Romans do anyway. For instance, you'll soon discover there's no point trying to toil round the sights in the afternoon heat, since most **8** of the museums and churches will be closed. Rather, this is the time to join the natives and seek the shade of palms and pines in one of Rome's parks, formerly the exclusive preserve of cardinals and princes, and now open to everyone.

Alternatively, you could sit soaking up the atmosphere in a tranquil piazza, admiring the play of sunlight on russet and ochre façades, listening to the water-music of the continually splashing fountains, and enjoying one of the refreshing drinks the Romans do so well: perhaps sip a cool *spremuta d'arancio* made from freshly squeezed blood oranges, or a creamy *frullato* fruit shake.

When the city re-awakens in the cool of the evening, join the Romans for their leisurely pre-dinner stroll, the *passeggiata*. This is the moment for greeting friends, exchanging news and, most importantly, checking out what everyone is wearing. One thing is certain: all the Romans will be dressed up to the nines.

The streets begin to thin out after 8pm, and this is your cue to find somewhere to go and eat. Remember that the finest Roman cuisine is based on the cooking of the poor; so your most memorable meal may well be found in a cosy restaurant in the old Jewish Ghetto or a traditional *trattoria* in the working-class district of Trastevere, rather than in a smarter establishment with a more swanky address.

Whichever way you decide to spend your stay in Rome, there will always be pleasant surprises in store. Don't feel you have to plan every step in advance; instead, copy the young English aristocrat who came to Rome on his Grand Tour in 1780 and decided to 'straggle and wander about just as the spirit chuses'.

Rome will always reward those who put their trust in serendipity.

A Brief History

Cherished legend claims that Rome was founded by Romulus, sired with twin brother Remus by Mars of a vestal virgin and abandoned on the Palatine Hill to be suckled by a she-wolf. Historians agree that the site and traditional founding date of 753 BC are just about right.

Archaeologists have further established that the site was occupied as early in history as the Bronze Age (c. 1500 BC) and that by the 8th century BC, villages had sprung up on the Palatine and Aventine hills and soon after on the Esquiline and Quirinal ridges. All these proved favourable spots for new settlements, as they were easily defensible and lay close to the midstream Isola Tiberina, which facilitated fording of the river.

After conquering their Sabine neighbours, the Romans merged the group of villages into a single city and surrounded it with a defensive wall, while the marshland below the Capitoline Hill was drained and became the Forum.

Under the consecutive rule of seven kings, the last three of whom were Etruscan, Rome

The River Tiber has been a witness to more than 2,700 years of Roman history.

began to develop as a powerful force in central Italy.

The Republic

A revolt by Roman nobles in 510 BC overthrew the last Etruscan king and established a Republic which was to last for the next five centuries. At first the young Republic, under the leadership of two patrician consuls, was plagued by confrontations between patrician and plebeian factions. But the plebs put forward their own leaders, the tribunes, to protect their interests, and therefore, strengthened internally, Rome began to expand its influence.

In 390 BC, the Gauls besieged the city for seven long

months, destroying everything but the citadel on the Capitoline Hill. When the Gauls left, the hardy citizens set about reconstructing, this time enclosing their city in a wall of huge tufa blocks. For over eight centuries, until the Barbarians came, no foreign invader was to breach those walls.

Rome now spread its control to all of Italy, consolidating its hold with six military roads fanning out from the city – Appia, Latina, Salaria, Flaminia, Aurelia and Cassia. By 250 BC, the city's population had grown to an impressive 100,000.

Victory over Carthage in the hundred years of Punic wars (264-146 BC) and conquests in Macedonia, Asia Minor, Spain and southern France extended Roman power in the Mediterranean. When Hannibal invaded Italy over the Alps in the Second Punic War, large areas of the peninsula were devastated and peasants sought refuge in Rome, swelling the population still further.

The acquisition of a largely unsought empire brought new

*T*he Colosseum (left) looms ma-
jestically over the ancient stones
of the Roman Forum (below).

social and economic problems to the Roman people. Unemployment, poor housing and an inadequate public works programme provoked unrest within the city. Violent civil wars shook the Republic, which ultimately yielded to dictatorship. Pro-consul Julius Caesar, who had achieved some fame by subduing Gaul and Britain, crossed the tiny Rubicon River marking the boundary of his province and marched boldly on Rome to seize power.

The Empire

Caesar's reforms, which bypassed the Senate in order to combat unemployment and to ease the tax burden, made dangerous enemies. His assassination on the Ides of March in 44 BC, led to a bitter civil war and the despotic rule of his adopted son Augustus, who became the first emperor. Under Augustus, the *Pax Romana* (Roman peace) reigned supreme over the far-flung empire. To make Rome a worthy capital, he added fine public buildings in the form of baths, theatres, and temples, claiming he had 'found Rome brick and left it marble'. He also introduced public services, including the first fire brigade. This was also the Golden Age of Roman Letters, distinguished by Horace, Ovid, Livy and Virgil.

In the first centuries of the empire, tens of thousands of foreigners flooded into Rome, among them the first Christians, including St Peter and St Paul. As this 'new religion' gained ground, the emperors tried to suppress it by means **13** of persecution, but the steadfastness of the martyrs only increased its appeal.

*M*arble fragments create a surreal statue of the Christian Emperor Constantine.

Each of Augustus's successors contributed his own embellishment to Rome. After a disastrous fire ravaged the city in AD 64, Nero rebuilt it and provided himself with an ostentatious palace, the Domus Aurea (Golden House), on the Esquiline Hill. Hadrian recon-

structed the Pantheon, raised a monumental mausoleum for himself (Castel Sant'Angelo) and retired to his magnificent estate, Villa Adriana at Tivoli.

In the late 1st and 2nd centuries AD, Rome reached the peak of its grandeur, with its population reaching over one million. Inherent flaws in the Imperial system, however, began to weaken the power of the emperors and led eventually to the total downfall of the empire.

After the death of Septimius Severus in AD 211, 25 emperors – all made and unmade by the armies - reigned in the short space of 74 years. Assassination was often the cause of the end of their reign. To add to the problems, fire and plague took their toll on the city's population, and in AD 283 the Forum was almost completely destroyed by fire – never to recover its former magnificence.

After a vision of the Cross appeared to him on a battlefield, Emperor Constantine then converted to Christianity, made it a state religion in AD 313 and built the first churches and basilicas in Rome. But in AD 331 he dealt a fatal blow to the empire's unification when he moved the Imperial seat to Byzantium (Constantinople). Many of the wealthy, as well as talented artists and artisans, went with him, a haemorrhage from which the old capital never recovered. Constantine's move effectively split the empire in two.

The Dark and Middle Ages

As the Western Empire went into decline, the Romans recruited Barbarians into the legions to help defend it against other outsiders. But the hired defenders soon joined the attackers, and the disenchanted and weary Roman populace failed to summon up the same enthusiasm to defend the city that they had shown in conquering an empire.

Wave after wave of dreaded Barbarians came to sack, rape, murder and pillage – Alaric the Visigoth in AD 410, Attila the Hun, the Vandals and the **15**

Ostrogoths. Finally the Barbarian chief, Odoacer, forced the last Roman emperor, Romulus Augustulus, to abdicate in AD 476. The Western Empire was at an end, although the Eastern Empire continued to prosper until 1453.

In the 6th century, Justinian reannexed Italy to his Byzantine Empire and codified Roman law as the state's legal system. But, as later Byzantine emperors lost interest, a new power arose out of the chaos in Rome: the Papacy. Pope Leo I (AD 440-461) had already asserted the Bishop of Rome as Primate of the Western Church and traced the succession back to St Peter; and Pope Gregory the Great (AD 590-604) had shown statesmanship in warding off the Lombards, a Germanic tribe already established in the north of Italy. In the 8th century, citing a document, the *Donation of Constantine* (later found to be a forgery), the popes began to claim political authority over all of Italy.

Rome by this time had been reduced to a village, with its small population (subsisting in the Tiber Marsh on the Campus Martius) deserting the hills when Barbarian invaders cut the Imperial aqueducts. Seeking the powerful support of the Franks, Pope Leo III crowned their king, Charlemagne, ruler of the Holy Roman Empire in St Peter's Basilica on Christmas Day AD 800. But the Pope had in turn to kneel in allegiance, and this exchange of spiritual blessing for military protection sowed the seeds of future conflict between popes and emperors.

Over the next 400 years, Italy saw invasions by Saracens and Magyars, Saxons and Normans (who were to sack Rome in AD 1084), with papal Rome struggling along as only one of many feudal city-states on the now tormented peninsula. The papacy, and with it Rome, was controlled by various powerful families from the landed nobility. As the situation in Rome degenerated into chaos – deplored by Dante in his *Divine Comedy* – the popes moved to comfortable exile in Avignon in 1309, and remained under the protection of the

HISTORICAL LANDMARKS

Earliest Beginnings
753 BC	Legendary founding of Rome.
510	Establishment of Republic.
390	Gauls sack the city.
264-146	Punic Wars against Carthage.
49	Julius Caesar seizes power.
44	Caesar assassinated in Rome.

Empire
27 BC	Augustus becomes first Roman emperor.
c. 64 AD	Persecution of Christians begins.
312	Constantine turns Christian.
331	Imperial capital moved to Byzantium.

Dark and Middle Ages
410	Visigoths sack Rome.
440-461	Pope Leo I asserts papal authority.
476	End of Western Roman Empire.
800	Pope crowns Charlemagne in St Peter's.
1084	Normans sack Rome.
1309-77	Popes exiled to Avignon.

Renaissance and Counter-Reformation
1508-12	Michelangelo paints Sistine Chapel ceiling.
1527	Sack of Rome by Imperial troops.
1798-1809	Napoleon's troops enter Rome and establish a Republic.
1814	Pope restored with Austrian rule.
1848	Italian nationalists revolt.
1861	Italy unified.
1871	Rome becomes capital of Italy.

Modern Era
1915	Italy enters World War I.
1922	Mussolini begins Fascist regime.
1929	Lateran Treaty creates separate Vatican state.
1940	Italy joins Germany in World War II.
1944	Allies liberate Rome.
1946	Monarchy abolished in favour of a Republic.

French king. Rome was left to the brutal rule of the Orsini and Colonna families.

A self-educated visionary, Cola di Rienzo, headed a popular revolution in 1347 and, anouncing himself Tribune of Rome, governed for a very brief seven months before the nobles finally drove him out.

The view from the dome of St Peter's Basilica is stunning, while down in St Peter's Square is a giant statue of St Paul (right).

The Renaissance

The popes, once re-established in Rome in 1377, harshly put down any resistance to their rule and remained dominant in the city for the next 400 years. Yet, during the 15th and 16th centuries, the papacy also became a notable patron of the Renaissance, that remarkable effusion of art and intellectual endeavour which gloriously transformed mediaeval Rome from a squalid, crumbling and fever-ridden backwater to the foremost city of the Christian world.

It was Giorgio Vasari, facile artist but first-rate chronicler of this cultural explosion, who dubbed it a *rinascita* or rebirth of the glories of Italy's Greco-Roman past. Furthermore, it proved, with the humanism of both Leonardo da Vinci and Michelangelo and the political realism of Machiavelli, to be the birth of our modern age.

The father of Rome's High Renaissance, Pope Julius II (1503-13), was responsible for the new St Peter's Basilica, and it was also he who commissioned Michelangelo to paint the ceiling of the Sistine Chapel and Raphael to decorate the Stanze. Donato Bramante, the architect, got the nickname *maestro ruinante* because of the countless ancient monuments he had dismantled for the Pope's megalomaniac building plans. With the treasures uncovered during this process, Julius founded the Vatican's magnificent collection of ancient sculpture.

The exuberant life of Renaissance Rome was brutally snuffed out in May 1527, however, by the arrival of mutinous troops of the invading German Emperor Charles V. It was to be the last – and worst – sack of the city.

Counter-Reformation

Meanwhile the position of the papacy and doctrines of the Church of Rome were being challenged by Luther, Calvin and other leaders of the Protestant Reformation.

The Counter-Reformation, formally proclaimed in 1563, reinforced the Holy Office's **19**

Inquisition to combat heresy and the Index to censor the arts. Italian Protestants fled and Jews in Rome were shut up in a ghetto.

Art proved a major instrument of Counter-Reformation propaganda. As the Church regained ground, it replaced the pagan influences of classicism with a more triumphant image, epitomized by Bernini's grand baroque altar canopy, which is to be found in St Peter's.

In the 18th century, Spain's authority over many of Italy's states passed to the Hapsburgs of Austria, who were determined to curb papal power in Rome. The papacy lost prestige with the enforced dissolution of the Jesuits, suffered a crippling loss of revenue from Hapsburg church reforms and finally sank to its lowest ebb.

In 1798 Napoleon's troops entered Rome, later seized the Papal States, and proclaimed a Republic. They treated Pius VI with contempt and carried him off to be a virtual prisoner in France. His successor, Pius VII, was forced to proclaim Napoleon as emperor and for his pains was also made prisoner, returning to Rome only after Napoleon was defeated in 1814.

During the French occupation, however, a national self-awareness began to develop among Italians to challenge the re-establishment of Austrian rule. Many people looked to Pope Pius IX to lead this nationalist movement, but he feared the spread of liberalism and held back. In 1848, when a Republic was set up in Rome by Giuseppe Mazzini in the name of Italian nationalism, the Pope fled. He returned only in the following year, after the Republic had been crushed by the French army.

National unity for Italy was achieved in 1860 through the shrewd diplomacy of Cavour, the Prime Minister, the heroics of guerrilla general, Giuseppe Garibaldi, and the leadership of King Vittorio Emanuele of Piedmont. Rome was captured by the nationalists in 1870 and became capital of Italy in the following year. Pope Pius IX retreated to the Vatican a 'prisoner of the monarchy'.

The Modern Era

In World War I Italy was on the winning side against Austria and Germany. But, after the peace conference of 1919, general disarray on the political scene led to an economic crisis, with stagnant productivity, bank closures and rising unemployment. Threatened by the Fascists' March on Rome in 1922, King Vittorio Emanuele III meekly invited their leader, *Il Duce* Benito Mussolini, to form a government.

Once firmly established in power, Mussolini made peace with the Pope by the Lateran Treaty of 1929, which created a separate Vatican state and perpetuated Catholicism as the national religion of Italy. In 1940 Mussolini plunged Italy into the Second World War on the side of the Germans. Rome was declared an open city to spare it from bombing and was liberated in 1944 with its treasures intact.

The initial post-war period was a time of hardship, but the 1950s saw Rome enjoying the fruits of Italy's 'economic miracle'. Jet-setting celebrities made the city their playground in the 1960s, finding *la dolce vita* in the nightspots of the Via Veneto.

Meanwhile, Rome's population was soaring, as poor immigrants from Italy's south flocked into the city in search of work. Speculative developers threw up whole suburbs of shoddy blocks of flats on the urban periphery.

The city weathered a storm of left- and right-wing political terrorism when the 1970s became Italy's *anni di piombo* ('years of lead'). The darkest hour came in 1978 when the Red Brigades kidnapped and murdered the Democrat Prime Minister, Aldo Moro.

As Rome now approaches the turn of another millenium, ancient monuments are being scrubbed clean while at the same time corruption scandals are revealing the somewhat dirty hands of the capital's politicians. Meanwhile, Romans get on with their daily lives, coping with the present, preparing for the future and preserving the past.

What to See

Visitors to Rome soon discover that the diverse eras which have influenced the city are often interwoven: thus a pagan mausoleum is also a papal fortress, a medieval church has a

In a city built on seven hills, you're never likely to be far from a splendid panoramic view.

baroque façade, and a Renaissance palace overlooks a modern traffic junction. It doesn't matter whether you've come to Rome for the grandeur of the ancient remains, the revered pilgrimage sites of the Catholic Church, or the inspired works of Michelangelo, Raphael and Bernini – you'll end up seeing aspects of them all anyway.

Although the municipality of Rome sprawls over a huge area, the principal sights are

packed into a comparatively small zone. The best way of getting about is on foot. Much of the historic centre has been closed to traffic, and driving elsewhere in the city can be hazardous for the uninitiated. Drivers are advised to leave their cars in a garage for the duration of their stay. Rome's public transport is often extremely crowded, but it will usually get you near enough to your destination. For the purpose of this guide we have grouped together places which can be most conveniently visited on the same walking tour.

Before you make a special trip to a museum or monument, it is best to check the current opening hours with the Tourist Office (see p.140) or your hotel, or look in the local newspapers (see p.130).

The Centro Storico

The heart of Rome's historic centre is the area enclosed by the bend of the River Tiber. Here, on what was once the

| **The Essentials** |
| For those making a brief visit to Rome, here are the very highest of the highlights: |
| ROMAN FORUM |
| CAMPIDOGLIO |
| COLOSSEUM |
| ST PETER'S BASILICA |
| VATICAN MUSEUMS |
| SPANISH STEPS |
| TREVI FOUNTAIN |
| PIAZZA NAVONA |
| PANTHEON |

Campus Martius, the 'Field of Mars' where Roman soldiers exercised, you will find vestiges of Rome's many different eras: the remains of ancient temples, a maze of medieval streets, graceful Renaissance palaces and ornate baroque churches, sublime piazzas and spectacular fountains. But it's up-to-date too – in amongst the monuments are the shops, hotels and businesses of modern Rome.

AROUND PIAZZA VENEZIA

Piazza Venezia is the most convenient place to begin an exploration of Rome's Centro Storico. The hub of the capital's main traffic arteries, this is not really a piazza in which to linger, but it is on several major bus routes and in close proximity to a number of interesting sites.

An added advantage, as far as orientation is concerned, is the presence of the massive **il Vittoriano** (Vittorio Emanuele Monument), a landmark visible from all over the city. Romans wish the dazzling white marble edifice were not quite so conspicuous, and heap upon it such derisive nicknames as 'Rome's False Teeth' and the 'Wedding Cake'. Built from 1885 to 1911 to celebrate the unification of Italy and dedicated to the new nation's first king, the Vittorio contains the tomb of Italy's Unknown Soldier of World War I.

A much more impressive work of architecture stands on the west side of the piazza: the **Palazzo Venezia**, the first great Renaissance palace in Rome. It was built for Cardinal Pietro Barbo, later Pope Paul II, supposedly so that he could watch the horse races along the Corso in comfort. Later it became the Embassy of the Venetian Republic to the Holy See, and this century served as Mussolini's official headquarters. His desk stood at the far corner of the vast Sala del Mappamondo in a move designed to intimidate visitors who had to approach across the full length of the marble floor. From the small balcony over the central door in the façade, *Il Duce* harangued his followers amassed in the square below. The palace now contains a museum of mediaeval and Renaissance furniture, arms, tapestries, ceramics and sculpture.

THE CAPITOLINE HILL

Two flights of steps lead up behind the Vittorio Emanuele Monument. The more graceful and gradual, known as La Cordonata, takes you up between colossal statues of the heavenly twins, Castor and Pollux, to the tranquil elegance of the **Campidoglio**, on top of the Capitoline Hill.

This was once the Capitol, where the Temple of Jupiter Optimus Maximus Capitolinus stood, the most sacred site of all in ancient Rome. Today the Campidoglio is the site of a glorious Renaissance square, due to the genius of Michelangelo, who designed the piazza, on the command of Pope Paul III, for the reception of the Holy Roman Emperor Charles V. Michelangelo also remodelled the existing **Palazzo Senatorio**, Rome's town hall down the ages, and planned the two palaces which flank it,

The First Capitol Hill

To the Romans, the Capitol was both citadel and sanctuary, the symbolic centre of government, where the consuls took their oath and the Republic's coinage was minted. Its name, now applied to many legislatures across the world (notably Congress in Washington), originated in a legend that the skull of a mythical hero was unearthed here during excavations for the Temple of Juno. Augurs interpreted this as a sign that Rome would one day be head (*caput*) of the world.

When the Gauls sacked Rome in 390 BC, the Capitol was saved by the timely cackling of the sanctuary's sacred geese, warning that attackers were scaling the rocks.

Later, victorious caesars ended their triumphal processions here. They rode up from the Forum in chariots drawn by white steeds to pay homage at the magnificent gilded Temple of Jupiter, which dominated the southern tip of the Capitoline.

In the Middle Ages, the collapsed temples were pillaged and the hill was abandoned to goats until, in the 16th century, Pope Paul III commissioned Michelangelo to give it new glory.

An impressive gallery in the Capitoline Museum, home to splendid works of art, statues and the Capitoline She-Wolf, symbol of Rome.

the Palazzo dei Conservatori and the Palazzo Nuovo, although other architects completed them after his death.

As a centrepiece, Michelangelo placed the magnificent gilded bronze **statue of Marcus Aurelius** in the square. The oldest equestrian bronze in the world, dating back to the 2nd century AD, it had survived because the pagan emperor had been mistaken for the Christian Constantine. So lifelike that, according to legend, Michelangelo commanded it to walk, the statue has recently emerged from a long period of restoration and is now displayed, behind glass, in the Palazzo Nuovo.

The Capitoline Museums, in the palaces of the Campidoglio, have extensive collections of magnificent sculpture excavated from ancient Rome. The

Palazzo Nuovo contains row upon row of portrait busts of Roman emperors, although its highlights are undoubtedly the poignant statue of the *Dying Gaul* and the sensual *Capitoline Venus*, a Roman copy of a Greek original dating from the 2nd century BC. In the courtyard of the **Palazzo dei Conservatori** you come across a giant marble head, hand and foot: fragments from a colossal statue of Emperor Constantine. The palace is also home to the famous **Capitoline She-Wolf**, an Etruscan bronze dating from around the 5th century BC, which has become the symbol of Rome. She is suckling the infants Romulus and Remus, Renaissance additions by Pollaiuolo. In a neighbouring room, note the beautifully poised bronze of a boy taking a thorn from his foot. The palace also houses the **Pinacoteca Capitolina** (Capitoline Picture Gallery), which has impressive works by Bellini, Titian, Velázquez, Rubens and Caravaggio.

Alongside the Palazzo Senatorio, a cobbled road opens out on to a terrace, giving you the first glimpse of the ruins of the Roman Forum (p.42), stretching from the Arch of Septimius Severus to the Arch of Titus, with the Colosseum beyond. On your right is the infamous Tarpeian Rock, from which the Romans hurled traitors to their deaths.

The steeper flight of steps up the Campidoglio climbs to the austere church of **Santa Maria in Aracoeli**, on the site of the great temple of Juno Moneta, where the Tiburtine Sibyl announced the coming of Christ to Augustus. The 13th-century church harbours the curious and much-revered Bambino, kept in a separate little chapel. Some Romans like to attribute miraculous healing powers to this statue of the infant Jesus, and stacks of unopened letters from all over the world addressed to Il Bambino surround the stumpy jewel-bedecked figure.

At Christmas the statue becomes the centrepiece of the manger scene, before which young children recite short poems and speeches. **27**

THE CORSO

The mile-long main street of central Rome runs in a straight line from Piazza Venezia to Piazza del Popolo. Known in ancient times as the *Via Lata*, the Corso derives its modern name from the carnival races or *corse* that were first held here in the 15th century under the spectacle-loving Venetian Pope Paul II. Of all the races, the most thrilling was the *Corsa dei Barberi*, in which riderless Barbary horses, sent into a frenzy by saddles spiked with nails, charged pell-mell along the narrow thoroughfare to be halted at last by a large white sheet hung across the street. Today the Corso is lined with palaces and churches, and crowded with shops and shoppers. Probably the busiest of Rome's streets, it is liveliest during the hour of the evening stroll or *passeggiata* (see p.9).

In the **Piazza Colonna**, the **column of Marcus Aurelius**, decorated with spiralling reliefs of the emperor's military triumphs, rises in front of the Italian prime minister's offices

in the Chigi Palace. The statue of the soldier-emperor, which originally stood on top of the column, was replaced in 1589 by a statue of St Paul.

On the **Piazza Montecitorio** next door, which is dominated by an Egyptian obelisk dating from the 6th century BC, stands the **Camera dei Deputati** (Chamber of Deputies), Italy's legislative lower house, designed by Bernini as a palace for the Ludovisi family.

If you turn off the Corso to the banks of the River Tiber, you can visit the **Ara Pacis Augustae**, a fascinating monument housed in a glass-sided building. When fragments of this 'Altar of Peace', commissioned to celebrate Augustus's victorious campaigns in Gaul and Spain, first came to light in 1568, they were dispersed among several European museums. The pieces were returned to Rome when reconstruction began earlier this century. Along the friezes you can make out Augustus himself, with his wife Livia and daughter Julia, friend Agrippa and a host of priests, nobles

Artists Galore

A host of artists and architects contributed to Rome's splendour. Here are some names that will crop up repeatedly during your visit, with examples of their most famous works in Rome.

ARNOLFO DI CAMBIO (c. 1245-1302). Gothic architect and sculptor from Pisa. Statue of St Peter in St Peter's Basilica, tabernacle in St Paul's.

BERNINI, GIANLORENZO (1598-1680). As painter, sculptor and architect, the foremost exponent of baroque art. St Peter's Square, Fountain of the Four Rivers, Palazzo Barberini.

BORROMINI, FRANCESCO (1599-1667). Baroque architect, assistant to and later great rival of Bernini. Sant'Agnese in Agone, Palazzo Barberini.

BRAMANTE, DONATO (1444-1514). Architect and painter from Urbino. Foremost architect of High Renaissance. St Peter's, Belvedere Courtyard in the Vatican.

CANOVA, ANTONIO (1757-1822). Most celebrated sculptor of the neo-classical movement. Statue of Napoleon's sister Pauline in the Borghese Gallery.

CARAVAGGIO, MICHELANGELO MERISI DA (1571-1610). Revolutionized art in the early 17th century. Paintings in Santa Maria del Popolo, San Luigi dei Francesi and Palazzo Barberini.

MADERNO, CARLO (1556-1629). Architect from northern Italy. Façade of St Peter's, papal palace at Castel Gandolfo.

MICHELANGELO BUONARROTI (1475-1564). Florentine painter, sculptor and architect, one of the most influential men in the history of art. Dome of St Peter's Basilica, Sistine Chapel ceiling, *Moses* in San Pietro in Vincoli, Campidoglio.

PINTURICCHIO, BERNARDINO (c. 1454-1513). Frescoes in Sistine Chapel, Borgia Apartments and Santa Maria del Popolo.

RAPHAËL (RAFFAELLO SANZIO) (1483-1520). Painter and architect of High Renaissance. Stanze in Vatican, Chigi Chapel in Santa Maria del Popolo, *La Fornarina* in Palazzo Barberini.

and dignitaries. Alongside the Altar, the great mound encircled by cypresses is the **Mausoleum of Augustus**, repository of the ashes of the caesars until Hadrian built his own mausoleum (now the Castel Sant'Angelo, see p.52) on the other side of the Tiber.

At its northern end, the Corso culminates in the graceful oval shape of the **Piazza del Popolo**, a truly exemplary piece of open-air urban theatre designed in 1818 by Giuseppe Valadier, former architect to Napoleon. The central obelisk, dating back to the Egypt of Ramses II (13th century BC), was brought to Rome by Augustus and erected in the Circus Maximus. Pope Sixtus V had it moved here in 1589.

The square takes its name from the Renaissance church of **Santa Maria del Popolo**, built on the site of Nero's tomb to exorcize his ghost, reputed to haunt the area. Its interior, remodelled for the baroque era, is famous for its works of art. They include an exquisite fresco of the *Nativity* by Pinturicchio, and Raphael's Chigi Chapel, built as a mausoleum for the family of the immensely rich Sienese banker and patron of the arts, Agostino Chigi. In the Cerasi Chapel, left of the choir, are two powerful canvases by Caravaggio, the *Conversion of St Paul* and *Crucifixion of St Peter*, notable for the dramatic use of light and shade and the masterly foreshortening of the figures.

Next to the church, the arched 16th-century **Porta del Popolo** marks the gateway to ancient Rome at the end of the Via Flaminia, which led from Rimini on the Adriatic Coast. Pilgrims arriving in Rome by the gate were greeted by the two imposing baroque churches of Santa Maria dei Miracoli and Santa Maria in Montesanto, both guarding the entrance to the Corso on the south side of the square.

To the east above the piazza, and reached by a monumental complex of terraces, the **Pincio** gardens offer a magical view of the city, especially at sunset, when the rooftops are tinged with purple and gold. Also the work of Valadier, the

30

gardens occupy the site of the 1st-century BC villa of Lucullus. This provincial governor returned enriched by the spoils of Asia and impressed his contemporaries by his extravagant lifestyle. The gardens stretch on into the less formal park of the **Villa Borghese**, once the estate of Cardinal Scipione Borghese, the nephew of Pope Paul V. The extensive grounds contain the Galleria Borghese (see p.86), housed in the cardinal's former summer palace, and a zoo to the north.

Lined with pine trees and open-air cafés, the Pincio promenade takes you past the **Villa Medici**, built in 1544 and bought by Napoleon as a home for the French National

The sweeping view from the Pincio captures one of Rome's finest squares, the Piazza del Popolo.

Academy. Today the villa is host to young French artists visiting Rome on scholarships.

AROUND THE PIAZZA DI SPAGNA

Now the city's most fashionable shopping district, the area around the **Piazza di Spagna** has been attracting foreigners for centuries. Aristocratic travellers on the Grand Tour came here, as did many of the most celebrated artists of the Romantic era, among them Keats (see below), Byron, Balzac, Wagner and Liszt.

The area continues to attract a cosmopolitan crowd. Well-heeled visitors come for the elegant and exclusive high-fashion shops along the Via Condotti and its neighbouring streets. Meanwhile, the more casually shod linger on the glorious **Scalinata della Trinità dei Monti** (the Spanish Steps), the city's most popular rendezvous for young Romans and foreigners alike. The steps ascend in three majestic tiers to the 16th-century church of **32** **Trinità dei Monti**, which,

with twin belfries and a graceful baroque façade, is one of Rome's most distinctive landmarks. Pink azaleas adorn the steps in spring and in summer they become the catwalk for an open-air fashion show at which top international designers present new eveningwear collections.

At the foot of the steps lies the **Fontana di Barcaccia**, a marble fountain in the shape of a leaking boat. The design, variously attributed to Pietro Bernini or his more famous son, Gianlorenzo, is an ingenious solution to the problem of low pressure in the Acqua Vergine which supplies the fountain with water.

The poet John Keats died in 1821 in a small room overlooking the steps. His house, 26 Piazza di Spagna, has since been preserved as the **Keats-Shelley Memorial** and museum. On the other side of the steps, at No. 23, the quintessentially English **Babington's Tea Rooms**, a pleasant oasis of Anglo-Saxon calm and gentility, has been serving tea and scones here since the 1890s, when it was opened by a Miss Babington along with her friend Miss Cargill.

An even more venerable establishment is found on nearby Via Condotti. **Caffè Greco** has been a favoured haunt of writers and artists for over two centuries, and the autographed portraits, busts and statues decorating the café attest to its distinguished clientèle, among them Casanova, Goethe, Baudelaire, Buffalo Bill, Gogol, and Hans-Christian Andersen.

Approached through a maze of narrow alleyways, the **Fontana di Trevi** (Trevi Fountain) never fails to astonish. Nicola Salvi's rococo extravaganza seems a giant stage-set, out of all proportion to its tiny piazza. The 18th-century fountain is in fact a triumphal arch and palace façade (for the old Palazzo Poli) which frames mythic creatures in a riot of rocks and pools. The centrepiece is the massive figure of Neptune, who rides on a sea-shell drawn by two winged sea horses led by tritons. The rearing horse symbolizes the sea's turmoil, the calm steed its tranquillity.

Marcello Mas... Anita Ekberg onc... memorably in the ... legendarily pure wate... they starred in Federico ... ni's film *La Dolce Vita*. authorities frown on that s... of behaviour today, but throw... a coin in over your shoulder...

Toss a coin into the Trevi Fountain, and it is said you will certainly return to Rome.

ensure a return

...ting the summit of ...est of the seven hills ...ent Rome is the baroque **zzo del Quirinale**. This ...s the summer palace of the ...opes until the unification of Italy in 1870, when it became home of the new King of Italy. Since 1947 it has been the offi-

cial residence of the President of the Republic. In the centre of the vast Piazza del Quirinale, magnificent **statues of Castor and Pollux** and their steeds, all Roman copies of Greek originals, stand beside an ancient obelisk. The piazza affords a splendid panoramic view over the whole city towards St Peter's.

Lovers of the baroque era will find much to delight them in this part of the city, which teems with masterpieces of sculpture and architecture by Bernini. Opposite the *manica*

*R*ome's historic *Caffè Greco has been the popular haunt of celebrities since 1760.*

34

lunga or 'long sleeve' of the Quirinal Palace you will find the small but perfectly formed church of **Sant'Andrea al Quirinale**, while in the nearby **Piazza Barberini** are two of the master's celebrated fountains: the **Fontana del Tritone**, which takes centre stage, and the **Fontana delle Api**, on its north side. Both fountains sport the bee symbol taken from the Barberini coat-of-arms of Pope Urban VIII, Bernini's patron.

The busy genius also had a hand in the architecture of the stately **Palazzo Barberini**, which now houses part of the Galleria Nazionale d'Arte Antica (see p.89).

A short distance away, but well worth the walk, is the church of **Santa Maria della Vittoria**, home to one of the supreme works of baroque sculpture, Bernini's *Ecstasy of St Theresa*. Based on a mystical vision experienced by Theresa of Avila, the statue shows the saint in the throes of a religious rapture that appears to be as much erotic as spiritual.

AROUND THE PIAZZA NAVONA

The **Piazza Navona** has been a prime spot for Roman recreation since the time of Emperor Domitian, who laid out an athletics stadium, *Circus Agonalis*, on the site in AD 79, establishing the future. square's oval shape.

Jousting tournaments took place here in the Middle Ages and from the 17th-19th century it was the scene of spectacular water pageants in summer, when the fountains overflowed until the piazza was flooded. As bands played, the aristocracy drove through the water in their gilded coaches, to the delight of onlookers. Today the piazza remains a colourful and lively spot. Sit at a pavement table of one of the cafés and enjoy the spectacle supplied by artists, buskers and quick-draw caricaturists.

The baroque centrepiece is Bernini's **Fontana dei Fiumi** (Fountain of the Four Rivers), which incorporates an ancient obelisk into a monumental allegory symbolizing the great **35** rivers of the Americas (Río de la Plata), Europe (the Danube), Asia (the Ganges) and Africa (the Nile). Romans who delight in Bernini's scorn for his rivals suggest that the Nile god is covering his head rather than have to look at Borromini's church of Sant'Agnese in Agone, and that the river god of the Americas is poised to catch it in case it collapses. In truth, the fountain was completed some years before Borromini's splendid – and indeed structurally impeccable – façade and dome.

The timeless grace and majesty of the **Pantheon**, in the Piazza della Rotonda, always impress visitors. The best-preserved monument of ancient

A Shocking Painter

Hot-tempered in life and a revolutionary in art, Michelangelo Merisi da Caravaggio single-handedly overturned the conventions of religious painting. His bold use of foreshortening and dramatic *chiaroscuro* have lost none of their force today, but it was his earthy realism that really shocked his contemporaries.

Caravaggio painted St Matthew with peasant hands and a wrinkled brow for the church of San Luigi dei Francesi near the Piazza Navona and was accused of irreverence. Furthermore, he was rumoured to have used a prostitute as the model for the Virgin Mary in his painting of the *Madonna of Loreto*, which hangs in the nearby church of Sant'Agostino. We know from the court records of the day that the prostitute, who plied her trade in Piazza Navona, was the cause of a quarrel in which Caravaggio wounded a notary in the summer of 1605.

A year later, the painter was forced to flee Rome after killing a man in a brawl that started over a game of racquets. There followed spells in Naples, Malta and Sicily and further scrapes with the authorities. He died of a fever in Port'Ercole in 1610, just as efforts were being made to gain him a pardon in Rome.

Rome, this 'Temple of all the Gods' was saved for posterity when it was converted into a church in the 7th century. The original Pantheon, built on this site in 27 BC by Marcus Agrippa, was destroyed by fire. Emperor Hadrian then rebuilt it around AD 125, but modestly left his predecessor's name on the frieze above the portico, which is supported by 16 monolithic pink and grey granite columns. The bronze beams which once adorned the entrance were taken away by the Barberini Pope Urban VIII to make Bernini's canopy for the high altar in St Peter's. His action prompted the saying: 'Quod non fecerunt barbari, fecerunt Barberini' ('What the Barbarians didn't do, the Barberini did').

The Pantheon's true greatness is only fully appreciated once you step inside and look up into the magnificent coffered dome. Over 43m (142ft) in diameter (exactly equal to its height), and even larger than the mighty cupola of St Peter's, the dome represents an unparalleled feat of archi-tecture and e... fine days a sha... lights up the wind... through the circular .... *lus*) in the dome (it ... in the rain). The gods an... desses are long gone, repl... by the Renaissance tombs ... Raphael and the architect Bal-dassare Peruzzi, as well as the modern kings Vittorio Emanuele II and Umberto I.

AROUND THE CAMPO DEI FIORI

The site of public executions during the 17th century, the **Campo dei Fiori** is now a bustling fruit and vegetable market. A reminder of the square's bloody past, however, is provided by the statue of philosopher Giordano Bruno, who was burned at the stake here by the Inquisition in 1600 for his heretical belief that the earth revolves around the sun, and not vice versa as the Church proclaimed.

An even more famous death occurred at the nearby Piazza del Biscione, or more precisely the restaurant Da Pancrazio,

...s the ruins of ...re where Julius ...ssassinated.

...at architects of the ...ked on the **Palazzo** ...se, Rome's finest Renaissance palace. Begun in ...14 by Antonio da Sangallo ...ne Younger for Cardinal Alessandro Farnese (Pope Paul III) Michelangelo then continued the project, and it was finally completed in 1589 by Giacomo della Porta. The building cost so much that it put a great strain on the fortune Farnese had amassed while he was Treasurer of the Church. Since 1871 the palace has been home to the French Embassy. You need special permission to see the ceremonial dining room's mythological frescoes by Annibale Caracci. Facing Palazzo Farnese, on the left of the square, is Palazzo Spada, a beautiful example of Renaissance art which houses a museum and art gallery.

The narrow streets heading south east of the Campo dei Fiori take you into the **Jewish Ghetto**, a lively and historic district peppered with restaur-

ants serving the city's distinctive Roman/Jewish cuisine. A feature of Roman life for more than 2,000 years, Jews were forced into a ghetto in the 16th century by Pope Paul IV. The walls that confined the quarter were torn down in 1848, but a small Jewish community still lives around the Via del Portico d'Otavia. The neo-Babylonian synagogue down by the river is linked to a museum of Jewish history.

One of the most charming fountains in Rome, the 16th-century **Fontana delle Tartarughe** (Turtle Fountain), can be found in Piazza Mattei. It depicts four boys perched on dolphins while lifting four turtles into a marble basin with gracefully outstretched arms.

A crumbling arched façade more than 2,000 years old, the **Portico d'Ottavia**, dedicated to Augustus' sister, once enclosed temples to Jupiter and Juno. Beyond it extends the **Teatro di Marcello** (Theatre of Marcellus), begun by Julius Caesar and the architectural model for the Colosseum.

The Ponte Fabricio, Rome's oldest bridge (62 BC), links the left bank to the **Isola Tiberina.** Three centuries before Christ the island was sacred to Aesculapius, god of healing, to whom a temple and hospital were dedicated. A hospital still stands here to this day, tended by the Brothers of St John of God. A second bridge, Ponte Cestio, remodelled in the 19th century, leads over to the right bank of the River Tiber and Trastevere (see p.41).

THE AVENTINE

Once revered as the 'Sacred Mount' in ancient times, when it stood outside Rome's walls, the Aventine remains a quiet sanctuary above the clamour of the city. An aristocratic district in the Imperial era, the hill is still a favoured residential zone, with villas and apartments set in shady gardens of flowers and palms.

Campo dei Fiori, the 'field of flowers', is the killing location for this colourful stall.

39

The Aventine is also the site of some of the earliest Christian churches, the most beautiful of which is the basilica of **Santa Sabina**. Here a classical harmony is given by the 24 white Corinthian columns lining the nave, while the beautiful carved cypress-wood doors in the portico contain one of the earliest depictions of the crucifixion in Christian art. The doors date back to the 5th century, as does the basilica itself. Through a window in the atrium you can see a descendant of an orange tree planted by St Dominic in 1220. A few steps away stands the villa of the Cavalieri di Malta (Knights of Malta. Take a peep through the keyhole of the garden door for an unusual view of the dome of St Peter's.

At the foot of the Aventine near the Tiber, the little church of **Santa Maria in Cosmedin** was given to Rome's Greek colony in the Middle Ages. Its Romanesque façade and simple interior provide stark contrast to the city's dominant baroque grandeur. Test your honesty in the portico's fierce-looking **Bocca della Verità** (Mouth of Truth). The ancient marble face is said to bite off the fingers of anyone with his hand in the gaping mouth who tells a lie.

Across the road, two of the city's most charming and best-preserved temples stand on what was once part of the ancient cattle-market. The one with fluted marble columns is erroneously known as the **Temple of Vesta** – probably dedicated to Hercules. Its rectangular neighbour, the **Temple of Fortune**, is a victim of the classical scholars' equivalent of a typing error, as its presiding deity is believed to have been Portunus, god of harbours, rather than Fortuna.

From the parapet of the Ponte Palatino, the mouth of the **Cloaca Maxima**, the great drain of ancient Rome, is visible at low tide. Begun by King Tarquin in around 600 BC, the sewer is still in use today.

South of the Aventine near Porta San Paolo, dark cypresses shade the beautiful **Protestant Cemetery** where Keats is buried (see p.32) and where

Shelley's ashes are interred. Towering over the cemetery is Rome's only **pyramid**, incorporated into the city walls. A Roman colonial magistrate, Caius Cestius, commissioned it for his tomb in 12 BC on his return from duty in Egypt.

TRASTEVERE

Trastevere has been Rome's traditional working-class quarter 'across the Tiber' (*Tevere*) since ancient times, and its inhabitants pride themselves on being the true Romans, a breed apart from the rest of the city. The word *Noiantri*, dialect for 'we others', reflects the way they see themselves, and is also the name for their riverside July festival of music and fireworks.

Despite recent gentrification which has dotted the district with smart shops, tearooms, clubs and restaurants , Trastevere still displays its lively atmosphere and idiosyncratic character, particularly in the narrow cobbled streets around the Piazza di Santa Maria, the heart of the quarter.

The church of **Santa Maria in Trastevere** is reputedly the oldest in the city. Its foundation (on the spot where oil is said to have gushed to presage the birth of Christ) can be traced back to the 3rd century, but the present structure dates from 1130-43 and is the work of Pope Innocent II, himself a Trasteverino. The façade is decorated with a beautiful and mysterious 12th-century mosaic of the Virgin flanked by ten maidens bearing lamps.

Before entering the church of **Santa Cecilia in Trastevere**, pause in the courtyard to admire the russet baroque façade and endearingly leaning Romanesque tower. Now regarded as the patron saint of music, St Cecilia was martyred for her Christian faith in AD 230. Her chapel stands over the site of the *caldarium* (bathhouse) in which she was tortured by scalding. The sculptor Stefano Maderno was on hand when her tomb was excavated in 1599 and his beautiful statue shows how the body then appeared, miraculously undecomposed.

41

lassical Rome

The nucleus of classical Rome is around the Colosseum (see p.49), with the Forum to the north west (see below) and the Baths of Caracalla (see p.50) to the south. Don't try to decipher each fragment of broken stone – not even archaeologists can do that. It's far better to soak up the romantic atmosphere while reflecting on the ruined majesty of this ancient civilization. Take care to avoid the midday sun in the shadeless Forum and finish your visit with a picnic and siesta on the Palatine.

THE ROMAN FORUM

With an exhilarating leap of the imagination, you can stand among the columns, porticoes and arches of the *Foro Romano* and picture the hub of the great Imperial city, the first in Europe to house a million.

Surrounded by the Palatine, Capitoline and Esquiline hills and drained by the Cloaca Maxima, an underground channel (see p.40), the flat valley of the Forum developed as the civic, commercial and religious centre of the growing city.

Under the emperors, it attained unprecedented splendour, with its white marble and golden roofs of temples, law courts and market halls glittering in the sun. After the Barbarian invasions, the area was abandoned. Subsequently fire, earthquakes, floods and the plunder of Renaissance architects reduced the area to a muddy cow pasture, until the excavations of the 19th century once again brought many of the ancient edifices to light. Grass still grows between the cracked paving stones of the Via Sacra, poppies bloom in among the piles of toppled marble and tangles of red roses are entwined in the brick columns, softening the harshness of the ruins.

Portable sound-guides can be rented at the entrance (on the Via dei Fori Imperiali) or you can find your own way round the Forum. But before you embark on this, a sensible move is to make yourself comfortable on a chunk of fallen

marble in the midst of the ruins and orient yourself, with the help of a detailed plan, so that you can trace the layout of the buildings and make sense of the apparent confusion.

Start your tour at the west end, just below the Campidoglio's Palazzo Senatorio (see p.25). Here you can see how the arches of the Roman record office (*Tabularium*) have been incorporated into the rear of the Renaissance palace. From here, look along the full length of the **Via Sacra** (Sacred Way), the route taken by victorious generals as they

The grandeur of ancient Rome survives in the majestic ruins of the Basilica of Maxentius.

rode in triumphal procession to the foot of the Capitoline Hill, followed by the legions' standards, massed ranks of prisoners and carts piled high with the spoils of conquest.

Then, to counterbalance this image of the Romans as ruthless military conquerors, turn to the severe brick-built rectangular **Curia**, home of the **43**

Roman Senate, in the north-west corner of the Forum. Here you can gaze through the bronze doors (copies of the originals which are now in the church of St John Lateran, see p.64) at the 'venerable great-grandmother of all parliaments', where the senators, robed in simple white togas, argued the affairs of Republic and Empire. It's worth noting that the tenets of Roman law, which underpins most Western legal systems, were first debated in this modest chamber.

Believed to mark the site of the very first assembly hall of the Roman elders, the Curia was constructed in its present form by Diocletian in AD 303. Its plain brick façade was once faced with marble. The church that covered it was dismantled in 1937 to reveal an ancient floor set with geometrical patterns in red and green marble, as well as the tiers on either side where the Roman senators sat, and the brick base of the golden statue of Victory at the rear. The Curia shelters two bas-reliefs, possibly from the Rostra (see below), outlining in marble the ancient buildings of the Forum.

In front of the Curia, a concrete shelter protects the underground site of the **Lapis Niger** (usually not on view), a black marble stone placed by Julius Caesar over the (presumed) grave of Romulus, the city's founder. Beside it is a stele engraved with the oldest Latin inscription ever found, dating back some six centuries before Christ; no one has completely deciphered it yet.

The triple **Arco de Settimio Severo** (Arch of Septimius Severus) dominates this end of the Forum. Its friezes depict the eastern military triumphs of the 3rd-century emperor who later campaigned as far as Scotland and died in York. Nearby is the orators' platform or **Rostra**, from which Mark Antony stirred the crowds into a frenzy after Julius Caesar's assassination. Its name comes from the iron prows (*rostra*), which once adorned it, taken from enemy ships at the Battle of Antium in 338 BC.

Two points have special significance: the *Umbilicus Urbis*

Romae, which marks the traditional centre of Rome, and the *Miliarium Aureum* (Golden Milestone), which recorded in gold letters the distances in miles from Rome to the provinces of the empire.

In front of the Rostra, public meetings and ceremonies took place in the social forum, kept bare save for samples of three plants essential to Mediterranean prosperity: the vine, the olive and the fig. Still prominent above this open space is the **Colonna di Foca** (Column of Phocas), built to honour the Byzantine emperor who presented the Pantheon to Pope Boniface IV.

Eight tall columns standing on a podium at the foot of the Capitol belong to the **Tempio di Saturno** (Temple of Saturn), one of the earliest temples in Rome. It doubled as both state treasury and centre of the December debauchery know as the Saturnalia, the pagan precursor of Christmas.

Of the **Basilica Julia**, once busy law courts, only the paving and some of the arches and travertine pillars survive. Even less remains of the Aemilia, on the oppos of the Via Sacra, destroy the Goths in AD 410.

Three slender columns, podium and a portion of the entablature denote the **Tempio dei Dioscuri** (Temple of Castor and Pollux), built 484 BC. It was dedicated to the twin sons of Jupiter (the Dioscuri) after they appeared on the battlefield at Lake Regillus to rally the Romans against the Latins and the Etruscans.

The altar of Julius Caesar is tucked away in a semi-circular recess of the **Tempio di Cesare** (Temple of the Divine Julius). On 19 March in 44 BC, the grieving crowds, following Caesar's funeral procession to his cremation in the Campus Martius, made an impromptu pyre of chairs and tables and burned his body in the Forum.

Pause for a pleasant idyll in the **Casa delle Vestali** (Hall of the Vestal Virgins), surrounded by graceful statues in the serene setting of a rose garden and old rectangular fountain basins, once more filled with water. In the circular white **45**

mpio di Vesta (the ... of Vesta), the sacred ... perpetuating the Roman ... was tended by six Vestal ...gins who, from childhood, ...bserved a 30-year vow of chastity under threat of being buried alive if they broke it. They were under the supervision of the high priest, the Pontifex Maximus (the popes have since appropriated this title) whose official residence was in the nearby Regia, of which only overgrown brick vestiges remain.

Further along the Via Sacra, the imposing **Temple of Antoninus and Faustina** has survived because, like the Curia, it was converted into a church, acquiring a baroque façade in 1602. In addition, few ancient buildings can match the massive proportions of the **Basilica of Maxentius**, completed by Constantine (whose name it also bears). Three giant vaults still stand.

The Via Sacra culminates in the **Arch of Titus**, built to commemorate the capture of Jerusalem in AD 70. Restored by Giuseppe Valadier in 1821, it shows in magnificent carved relief the triumphal procession of Titus bearing the spoils of the city, among them the Temple of Jerusalem's seven-branched golden candlestick and silver trumpets which later vanished, possibly in the sack

*G*raceful statues of ancient Rome's maiden princesses line the Hall of the Vestal Virgins.

of Rome by the Vandals. Even today, many Jews will avoid walking through the arch that glorifies their tragedy.

From this end of the Forum a slope leads up to the **Palatine Hill**, Rome's legendary birthplace and today its most romantic garden, dotted with toppled columns among the wild flowers and spiny acanthus shrubs. At the time of the Republic, this was a desirable residential district for the wealthy and aristocratic, with Cicero and Crassus among its distinguished inhabitants.

Augustus began the Imperial trend and later emperors added and expanded, each trying to oudo the last in magnificence and luxury until the whole area was one immense palace (the very word takes its name from the hill). From the pavilions and terraces of the 16th-century botanic gardens laid out here by the Farnese family, there is an excellent view of the whole Forum.

The so-called **House of Livia** is now believed to be that of her husband, Emperor Augustus, who here combined modesty with taste. Small, graceful rooms retain remnants of mosaic floors and a well-preserved wall painting which depicts Zeus' love for a young priestess. Nearby, a circular Iron Age dwelling unearthed from the time of Rome's legendary beginnings is known as **Casa di Romolo** (Romulus' Hut).

A subterranean passageway linking the palaces, the **Cryptoporticus of Nero**, threads through the Palatine. In the dim light you can just make out stucco decorations on the ceilings and walls. The vast assemblage of ruins of the *Domus Flavia* include a basilica, throne room, banqueting hall, baths, porticoes and a fountain in the form of a maze. Together with the *Domus Augustana*, the complex is known as the **Palace of Domitian**. From one side you can look down into the **Stadium of Domitian** which was probably a venue for horse races, but thought by some to have been a sunken garden.

The last emperor to build on the Palatine, Septimius **47**

Severus, carried the Imperial palace right to the south-eastern end of the hill, so that his seven-storeyed **Domus Severiana** was the impressive first glimpse of the capital for new arrivals. It was dismantled to build Renaissance Rome, and only the huge arcaded fountains remain.

From this edge of the Palatine you have a splendid view down into the immense grassy stretch of the **Circus Maximus**, where crowds of up to 200,000 watched chariot races from tiers of marble seats.

The **Imperial Forums** were built as an adjunct to the *Foro Romano* in honour of Julius Caesar, Augustus, Trajan, Vespasian and Nerva. The most impressive monument is the 30m (98ft) **Trajan's Column** (AD 113). Celebrating Trajan's campaigns against the Dacians in what is now Romania, the minutely detailed friezes spiralling round the Column constitute a veritable textbook of

---

Seeing the Pope

When he's not in Bogotá or Bangkok, it is possible to see the Pope in person at his personal residence, the Vatican. He normally holds a public audience every Wednesday at 11am (10am in summer), either in a large modern audience hall or down in St Peter's Square (and sometimes at his summer residence at Castel Gandolfo). An invitation to a papal audience may be obtained from the Pontifical Prefect's Office (open Monday to Saturday in the morning) through the bronze gates in St Peter's Square. A visitor's bishop at home can arrange a private audience.

On Sundays at noon, the Pope appears at the window of his apartments in the Apostolic Palace (right of the basilica, overlooking the square), delivers a brief homily, says the Angelus and blesses the crowd below. On a few major holy days, the pontiff celebrates high mass in St Peter's.

Roman warfare, featuring embarkation on ships, the clash of armies and the surrender of Barbarian chieftains. St Peter's statue replaced the emperor's in 1587.

THE COLOSSEUM

It says something about the essential earthiness of Rome that, more than any inspirational church or palace, it is the **Colosseum** – Byron called it 'the gladiator's bloody circus' – that is the symbol of the city's eternity. Built in AD 72-80 by 20,000 slaves and prisoners, the four-tiered elliptical amphitheatre seated 50,000 spectators on stone benches, according to social status.

Flowing in and out of 80 arched passageways known as *vomitoria*, aristocrat and plebeian alike came to see blood: bears, lions, tigers and leopards starved into attacking one another; trained fighters slaying animals; gladiators butchering one another to cries of '*Jugula!*' ('Slit his throat!'). The gladiators were originally criminals, war captives and slaves; later, free men entered the 'profession', tempted by wealth and fame. Contrary to popular belief, there is little historical evidence to support the image of the Colosseum as the place where Christians were fed to the lions.

Popes and princes have since stripped the Colosseum of its precious marble, travertine and metal for their churches and palaces. They have left behind a ruined maze of cells and corridors which funnelled both men and beasts to the slaughter. The horror has disappeared beneath the moss, but the thrill of the monument's endurance remains. As an old Anglo-Saxon prophecy goes: 'While stands the Colosseum, Rome shall stand; when falls the Colosseum, Rome shall fall; and when Rome falls with it shall fall the world.'

The nearby **Arch of Constantine** celebrates Constantine's victory over his Imperial rival Maxentius at the Mulvian Bridge. He may have won the battle, but a cost-conscious Senate took fragments from monuments of earlier rulers, **49**

*W*ild beasts once fought in the Colosseum's mighty arena – today feral cats make it their home.

Trajan, Hadrian and Marcus Aurelius to decorate the arch.

Heading south of the Colosseum 1km (½mile), the huge 3rd-century **Terme di Caracalla** (Baths of Caracalla) were built for 1,600 people to bathe in considerable style and luxury. Imagine these impressive brick walls covered in coloured marble. Public bathing was a prolonged social event as merchants and senators passed from the *caldarium* (hot room) to cool down in the *tepidarium* and the *frigidarium*. The baths ran dry in the 6th century when Barbarians cut the aqueducts. Now the stage for spectacular open-air operas in the summer, the *caldarium* is vast enough for processions of elephants, camels and four-horse chariots.

The Vatican

The power of Rome endures both in the spirituality evoked by every stone in St Peter's Basilica and in the physical awe inspired by the splendours of the Vatican palace. At their best, the popes and cardinals replaced military conquest by moral leadership and persuasion; at their worst, they could show the same hunger for political power and wealth as any caesar. A visit to the Vatican is an object lesson for faithful and sceptic alike.

Constantine, first Christian emperor, erected the original St Peter's Basilica over an oratory on the site of the Apostle's tomb in AD 324. After it was sacked in AD 846 by marauding Saracens, Pope Leo IV ordered massive walls to be built around the sacred church, and the enclosed area became known as the Leonine City – and later the Vatican City, after the Etruscan name of its hill.

The Vatican became the main residence of the popes only after 1378 when the papacy was returned to Rome from exile in Avignon (see p.16). It has been a sovereign state, independent of Italy, since the Lateran Pact signed with Mussolini in 1929. The Pope is supreme ruler of this tiny state, which is guarded by an elite corps of Swiss Guards, founded in 1506, who still wear the blue, scarlet and orange uniforms said to have been designed by Michelangelo. The papal domain has its own newspaper, *L'Osservatore Romano*, and a radio station which broadcasts worldwide. It also has shops, banks, a minuscule railway station (rarely used) and a post office that will get your postcards home far more quickly than the Italian postal service.

Apart from the 1sq km (½sq mile) comprising St Peter's Square, St Peter's Basilica and the papal palace and gardens, the Vatican also has jurisdiction over other, extra-territorial, enclaves, including the basilicas of St John Lateran, Santa Maria Maggiore and St Paul's as well as the Pope's summer residence at Castel Gandolfo (see p.96).

51

You don't need a passport to cross the border, and in fact you hardly even notice that you have – though it is marked by a band of white travertine stones running from the ends of the two colonnades at the rim of St Peter's Square. The Vatican Tourist Information Office on St Peter's Square arranges guided tours and issues tickets to the grounds of the Vatican City, including the gardens. From here buses go regularly, bound for the Vatican Museums.

A visit to St Peter's combines ideally with a tour of the Castel Sant'Angelo, culminating in a picnic and siesta on the nearby Janiculum Hill. It is best to save the Vatican Museums for a separate day.

CASTEL SANT'ANGELO

Cross the Tiber by the **Ponte Sant'Angelo**, which incorporates arches of Hadrian's original bridge, the Pons Aelius. Ten windswept angles designed by Bernini, each bearing a symbol of the Passion of Christ, adorn the balustrades.

From the bridge you have the best view of the cylindrical bulk of the **Castel Sant'Angelo**, its mighty brick walls stripped of their travertine and pitted by cannonballs, but nevertheless standing up well to the ravages of time. Conceived by Hadrian around AD 130 as his family mausoleum, it became part of the defensive Aurelian Wall a century later. The castle gained its present name in AD 590 after Pope Gregory the Great had a vision of the Archangel Michael alighting on a turret and sheathing his sword to signal the end of a plague. For centuries this was Rome's mightiest military bastion and a refuge for the popes in times of trouble; Clement VII holed up here during the sack of Rome by Hapsburg troops in 1527.

A spiral ramp, showing traces of the original black and white mosaic paving, leads up to the funerary chamber where the Imperial ashes were kept in urns. You emerge into the **Cortile dell'Angelo** (Court of the Angel), which is stacked neatly with cannonballs and watched over by a marble angel. An arms museum opens off the courtyard.

After the grimness of the exterior, it comes as a surprise to step into the luxurious surroundings of the old **Papal Apartments**. Lavish frescoes cover the walls and ceilings of rooms hung with masterpieces by Dosso Dossi, Nicolas Poussin and Lorenzo Lotto. Off the Courtyard of Alexander VI is possibly the most exquisite bathroom in history. The tiny room, just wide enough for its marble bathtub, is painted with delicate designs over every inch of its walls and along the side of the bath.

A harsh jolt brings you back to reality as you enter the **dungeons**, scene of torture and executions. You have to bend over double to get into the bare, stone cells where famous prisoners languished – among them sculptor-goldsmith Benvenuto Cellini and philosopher Giordano Bruno.

*I*n times of crisis, beleaguered popes took refuge behind the stout walls of the Castel Sant'Angelo.

53

The **Gallery of Pius IV**, surrounding the entire building, affords tremendous views in all directions, as does the terrace on the summit, by the 18th-century bronze *Statue of St Michael* by Verschaffelt. Opera lovers will recall this as the stage for the final act of Puccini's *Tosca*, in which the heroine hurls herself to her death from the battlements.

ST PETER'S

From the Castel Sant'Angelo a wide straight avenue, the Via della Conciliazione, leads triumphantly up to St Peter's. A maze of medieval streets, in which stood Raphael's studio, was destroyed in the 1930s to provide an unobstructed view of St Peter's all the way from the banks of the Tiber. A thick wall running parallel to the avenue conceals a passageway (*Il Passetto*) linking the Vatican to the Castel Sant'Angelo, by which the fleeing popes reached their bastion in safety.

In **Piazza San Pietro** (St Peter's Square), his greatest creation, Bernini managed to

conceive one of the world's most exciting pieces of architectural orchestration.

The sweeping curves of the colonnades reach out to Rome and the whole world, *urbi et orbi*, to draw the flood of pilgrims into the bosom of the church. On Easter Sunday as many as 300,000 people cram into the piazza. The square is on or near the site of Nero's circus, where early Christians were martyred.

Bernini completed the 284 travertine columns and 88 pilasters topped by 140 statues of the saints in just 11 years, from 1656-67. In the centre of the ellipse rises a 25m (84ft) red granite **obelisk**, brought here from Egypt by Caligula in AD 37. Stand on one of the two circular paving stones set between the obelisk and the twin 17th-century fountains to see the quadruple rows of perfectly aligned Doric columns appear magically as one.

By any standards a grandiose achievement, **St Peter's Basilica** does inevitably suffer from the competing visions of all the architects called in to collaborate – Bramante, Baldassare Peruzzi, Giuliano da Sangallo, Carlo Maderno, Giacomo della Porta, Raphael, Michelangelo and Domenico Fontana, each of whom added, subtracted and modified, often with a Pope over his shoulder.

From 1506, when the new basilica began under Julius II, until 1626 when it was consecrated, St Peter's Basilica was to change form several times. It started out as a simple Greek cross, with four arms of equal length, as favoured by Bramante and Michelangelo, and ended up as Maderno's Latin

Today the duties of the Swiss Guards at the Vatican are more ceremonial than military.

cross extended by a long nave, as demanded by the popes of the Counter-Reformation. One result is that Maderno's porticoed façade and nave obstruct a clear view of Michelangelo's dome from the square.

Stepping into the basilica is 'like entering eternity', according to the poet, Goethe. The world's largest Catholic church certainly has immense dimensions: 212m (695ft) long on the outside, 187m (613ft) inside, and 132m (435ft) to the tip of the dome. Brass markers on the floor of the central aisle show how far other famous cathedrals fail to measure up.

You'll find the basilica's most worthy artistic treasure, Michelangelo's sublime *Pietà*, in its own chapel to the right of the entrance. The artist was only 24 when he executed this deeply moving marble sculpture of the Virgin cradling the crucified Christ in her lap. This is the only work which he bothered to sign (on the Madonna's sash), after overhearing people crediting it to another sculptor. Since it was attacked by a religious fanatic with a hammer in 1972, the statue has been protected by a glass screen.

Reverence can also cause damage: on the 13th-century bronze *Statue of St Peter*, a work of the Florentine architect-sculptor Arnolfo di Cambio, the toes have been worn away by the lips and fingers of countless pilgrims.

Beneath the dome, Bernini's great *baldacchino* (canopy) soars over the high altar, at which only the Pope may celebrate mass. The canopy and four spiralling columns were cast from bronze beams taken from the Pantheon (see p.36). Notice at the bottom of each column the coat of arms bearing the three bees of the Barberini Pope Urban VIII, who commissioned the work. In the apse is an even more extravagant baroque work, Bernini's bronze and marble *Cathedra of St Peter*, throne of the Apostle's successors, into which is supposedly incorporated the wooden chair of St Peter.

For his imposing **dome**, Michelangelo drew inspiration from the Pantheon (see p.36) and the cathedral in Florence. A lift takes you as far as the gallery above the nave from where there is a dizzying view down into the interior of the basilica, as well as close-ups of the inside of the dome. Spiral stairs and ramps lead on and up to the outdoor balcony which circles the top of the dome for stunning views of the Vatican City and all Rome.

The **Vatican Grottoes** beneath the basilica harbour the tombs of popes and numerous little chapels, some decorated by such masters as Melozzo da Forlì, Giotto and Pollaiulo. The **necropolis**, even deeper underground, shelters several pre-Christian tombs, as well as a simple monument which may have marked St Peter's burial place. This excavated area is not open to general viewing and visits should be arranged in advance through the Ufficio Scavi, through the Arco della Campana to the left of the basilica.

St Peter's is open daily from 7am to 6pm (until 7pm from June to September). Masses are said frequently in the side chapels, in various languages. Visitors wearing shorts, barebacked dresses or other scanty attire are politely turned away.

VATICAN MUSEUMS

It should come as no surprise that the Catholic Church, as the greatest patron that painters, sculptors and architects have known, should have in its headquarters one of the richest collections of art in the world. The 7km (4 miles) of rooms and galleries of the **Vatican Museums** offer a microcosm of Western civilization. There is an almost bewildering profusion, from Egyptian mummies, Etruscan gold jewellery and Greek and Roman sculpture, through Renaissance and medieval masterpieces to modern religious art. On a single ticket you can visit eight museums, five galleries, the Apostolic Library, Borgia Apartments, Raphael Rooms and, of course, the Sistine Chapel.

Once past the entrance, you ascend a wide spiral ramp, and then choose between four colour-coded itineraries which **57**

range from 1½ hours (A, violet) to 5 hours (D, yellow). The following gives a selection of some of the highlights.

With the booty from the ruthless dismantling of ancient monuments to make way for the Renaissance city in the 16th century, the **Museo Pio-Clementino** has assembled a wonderful collection of classical art. The most celebrated piece is the 1st-century BC *Laocoön* group of the Trojan priest and his sons, who were strangled by serpents for offending Apollo. Famous during Imperial times, it was unearthed from a vineyard on the Esquiline in 1506, to the delight of Michelangelo, who rushed to view it. It now stands in a recess of the charming octagonal Belvedere courtyard.

Roman copies of some other Greek sculptures, such as the *Aphrodite of Cnidos* of Praxiteles and the superb *Apollo Belvedere*, achieved a fame as great as the originals, which are now sadly lost. Take note in particular of the powerful muscular *Torso* by Apollonius, **58** which had a profound influ-

ence on Renaissance artists and sculptors.

The **Gregorian-Etruscan Museum** displays the exciting finds from a 7th-century BC Etruscan burial mound at Cerveteri (see p.96), whose tomb yielded an abundance of treasures. Among the fine jewellery is a gold brooch surprisingly decorated with lions and ducklings. Look out for the striking bronze statue of a sprightly Etruscan warrior, the *Mars of Todi* (4th century BC).

Judging by the number of obelisks scattered throughout Rome, Egyptian art was much admired and sought after by the ancient Romans. The basis of the collection in the **Egyptian Museum** rests on finds from Rome and its surroundings, particularly from the Gardens of Sallust between the Pincian and Quirinal hills, the Temple of Isis on the Campus Martius and Hadrian's Villa at Tivoli (see p.93). One of the rooms recreates the underground chamber of a tomb in the Valley of the Kings.

Pope Julius II took a calculated risk in 1509 when he

In mile after mile of halls and galleries, the Vatican Museums display some of the greatest artistic treasures of the Western world.

called in a relatively untried 26-year-old to decorate his new residence. The result was the four **Stanze di Raffaello** (Raphael Rooms). In the central Stanza della Segnatura are the two masterly frescoes, *Disputation over the Holy Sacrament* and the *School of Athens*, which contrasted theological and philosophical wisdom.

The *Disputation* unites biblical figures with historical pillars of the faith such as Pope Gregory and Thomas Aquinas, but also painter Fra Angelico and the divine Dante. At the centre of the *School*, Raphael is believed to have given the red-robed Plato the features of Leonardo da Vinci, while portraying Michelangelo as the thoughtful Heraclitus, seated in the foreground.

For a stark contrast to Raphael's grand manner, seek out **59** the gentle beauty of Fra Angelico's frescoes in the **Cappella del Beato Angelico** (Chapel of Nicholas V). The lives of Saints Lawrence and Stephen are told in delicately subdued pinks and blues, highlighted with gold.

The richly decorated **Borgia Apartments** contain Pinturicchio's sublime frescoes, with portraits of lusty Pope Alexander VI, his notorious son Cesare and daughter Lucrezia, and lead into the modern religious art collection of Paul VI. This includes Matisse's Madonna sketches, Rodin bronzes, Picasso ceramics, designs for ecclesiastical robes and, somewhat unexpectedly, a grotesque Pope by Francis Bacon.

One of Europe's finest collections of ancient manuscripts and rare books is kept in the hallowed precincts of the **Apostolic Library**. In the great vaulted reading room, or Sistine Hall, designed by Domenico Fontana in 1588, walls and ceilings are covered with paintings of ancient libraries, conclaves, thinkers and writers. Showcases displaying precious illuminated manuscripts have replaced the old lecterns.

Working Solo on the Ceiling

As might be imagined, painting the Sistine ceiling wasn't easy. Michelangelo, a sculptor who used marble and had only a limited experience of oil painting, had never before produced a fresco. Preferring his inexperience to their incompetence, he fired his seven assistants in the first couple of weeks and continued alone for four years, from 1508-12. Contrary to legend, he did not lie on his back, but painted erect on tiptoe, bent backwards 'like a Syrian bow', with Pope Julius II climbing the scaffolding to check on progress and threatening to throw him off his platform if he didn't hurry up.

'I'm not in a good place,' he wrote to a friend, 'and I'm no painter.'

A 1,600-year-old copy of Virgil's works, the poems of Petrarch, a 6th-century gospel of St Matthew, and Henry VIII's love letters to Anne Boleyn are among the prize possessions.

Nothing can prepare you for the visual shock of the **Cappella Sistina** (Sistine Chapel), built for Sixtus IV in the 15th century. Despite the distracting presence of the crowds, visitors seem to yield to the power of Michelangelo's ceiling, his *Last Judgement*, as well as the other wall frescoes of Botticelli, Rosselli, Pinturicchio, Ghirlandaio and Sig-

norelli. In this private papal chapel, where cardinals hold their conclave to elect the new Pope, the glory of the Catholic Church achieves its finest artistic expression.

The chapel portrays nothing less than the story of man, in three parts: from Adam to Noah; the giving of the Law to Moses; and from the birth of Jesus to the Last Judgement. Towards the centre of the ceiling, you can make out the celebrated outstretched finger of the *Creation of Adam*. Most overwhelming of all, particularly now that the colours are

so fresh and vivid after a recent restoration, is the impression of the whole. This is best appreciated looking back from the bench by the chapel's exit.

On the chapel's altar wall is Michelangelo's tempestuous *Last Judgement*, painted 23 years after the ceiling, when the artist was in his sixties, and imbued with profound religious soul-searching. An almost naked Jesus dispenses justice more like a stern, even fierce classical god-hero than the conventionally gentle biblical figure. The artist's agonizing self-portrait can be seen in the flayed skin of St Bartholomew, below Jesus.

Amid all the Vatican's treasures, the 15 rooms of the **Pinacoteca Vaticana** (Picture Gallery), in a separate wing of the palace, sometimes get short shrift. Among the most important exhibits in this collection, covering ten centuries of painting, are works by Fra Angelico, Perugino, Raphael's *Transfiguration* (his last great work), Leonardo da Vinci's unfinished *St Jerome* in sombre tones of sepia, Bellini's

Pietà, and Caravaggio's *Descent from the Cross*.

As you wander the galleries, glance out of the windows from time to time to view St Peter's dome over the clipped hedges of the Vatican gardens (the best views are from the Gallery of the Maps). Take a rest in the **Cortile della Pigna**, dominated by the enormous bronze pine-cone fountain (1st century AD) which gives the courtyard its name.

THE JANICULUM

After absorbing the riches of the Vatican, you could be forgiven for suffering a severe case of cultural overload. Rising above the Vatican, the Janiculum Hill provides prescribed respite in the shade of its parks. From the crest, there is a breathtaking view of Rome from the **Piazzale Garibaldi**. In the centre of the square is an equestrian statue of the hero of the Risorgimento, who fought a fierce battle here in 1849. From the crest the road winds down into Trastevere (see p.41).

Churches

It's impossible to list – much less visit – all the churches in Rome. There are some 280 within the centre of the city: far more than even the most zealous of pilgrimages can encompass. Students of history and art, as well as pilgrims, aim to visit the four patriarchal basilicas: St Peter's (see p.54), Santa Maria Maggiore, St John Lateran and St Paul's Outside the Walls.

Some churches have relics of saints and martyrs to make them special sites, others are significant landmarks in the development of Western architecture, and many more contain magnificent works of art. Here is a representative selection of the best.

Gold from the New World adorns the splendid, coffered ceiling of the church of Santa Maria Maggiore

 SANTA MARIA MAGGIORE

This largest and most splendid of all the churches dedicated to the Virgin Mary was first built in the 4th century by Pope Liberius over the site of a Roman temple dedicated to the goddess Juno on the Esquiline Hill. A century later it was torn down and rebuilt by Sixtus III.

Glittering **mosaics** enhance the perfect proportions of the interior. Above the 40 ancient Ionic columns of the triple nave, a mosaic frieze portrays Old Testament scenes leading to the coming of Christ. The theme is continued in the gilded Byzantine-style mosaics on the triumphal arch, detailing the birth and the childhood of Jesus, and culminates in the magnificent 13th-century portrayal of Mary and Jesus enthroned, in the apse behind the high altar. Inlaid red and green precious marbles pattern the floor in the cosmatesque style first pioneered by Rome's Cosmati family of craftsmen during the 12th century.

Note the opulence of the coffered **Renaissance ceiling**, gilded with the first shipment of gold from the Americas. A casket of gold, silver and crystal contains fragments reputed to have come from the holy crib, brought back from the Holy Land by St Helena, Constantine's mother.

The incomparably rich **Capella Paolina** (Pauline Chapel) has an altar inlaid with agate, amethyst and lapis lazuli set beneath a revered 9th-century painting of the Madonna and Child. On 5 August, white petals are showered on the altar to mark the date when a miraculous fall of snow, prophesied by the Virgin, showed Pope Liberius where to build the church.

ST JOHN LATERAN

Regarded as the mother church of the Catholic world (it's the seat of the Pope as Bishop of Rome), **San Giovanni in Laterano** pre-dated even the first St Peter's by a few years. Constantine built both basilicas in the early 4th century.

A Selection of Hotels and Restaurants in Rome

Recommended Hotels

If you are travelling independently you might like to try one of the following hotels recommended by Berlitz. Italian hotels are classified by the government from five stars down to one star according to the facilities they offer. However, the star rating does not give a guide to the character or location of the hotel. As prices do not always include breakfast we recommend that you check this when you book. As a basic guide we have used the symbols below to indicate prices for a double room with bath or shower, including service charge, tax and VAT:

	below L150,000
	L150,000-250,000
	above L250,000

Aldrovandi Palace |||
(Parioli)
Via Ulisse Aldovrandi, 15, 00197
Tel. 3223993
Fax 3221435
Old World style and service with many amenities, including pool, garden and the Relais la Piscine restaurant. 139 rooms.

Ambasciatori Palace |||
(Via Veneto)
Via Vittorio Veneto 70, 00187
Tel. 47493
Fax 4743601
Luxury hotel designed in 1927 by Marcello Piacentini. In the lobby are great frescoed murals depicting the *beau monde* of the 1920s. Still faithful to its pre-

Depression grandeur in service and style. 149 rooms.

Arenula |
(Ghetto)
Via Santa Maria dei
Calderai 47, 00186
Tel. 6879454
Fax 6896188
A comfortable and reasonably-priced cheap hotel in the heart of the Ghetto. 37 rooms.

Atlante Star |||
(near St Peter's)
Via Vitelleschi 34, 00193
Tel. 6879558/6873233
Fax 6872300
Modern hotel with a spectacular view of St Peter's from its roof-

garden restaurant, Les Etoiles. 61 rooms.

Barrett

(near Largo Argentina)
Via di Torre Argentina 47, 00186
Tel. 6868481
Tiny, central and comfortable for the price. 15 rooms.

Brittania

(near Termini Station)
Via Napoli 64, 00184
Tel. 4883153/4885785
Comfortable hotel with plenty of amenities such as television, minibar, room safe and hair dryer all included in the very moderate price. 32 rooms.

Campo De' Fiori

(near Campo de' Fiori)
Via del Biscione 6, 00186
Tel. 6874886
Economical hotel in Rome's historic centre. Good views of the whole of the city from the rooftop terrace. 27 rooms.

Carriage

(Corso/Piazza di Spagna)
Via delle Carrozze 36, 00187
Tel. 6990124
Fax 6788279
Quiet hotel near the Spanish Steps with 27 pleasant, well-furnished rooms.

Cavalieri Hilton

(Monte Mario)
Via A Cadlolo 101, 00136
Tel. 35091
Fax 35092241
A peaceful location away from the centre with splendid views from Monte Mario. Outdoor swimming pool, terrace, park, tennis. Outdoor dining. 377 rooms.

Cesari

(near Corso)
Via di Pietra 89/a, 00186
Tel. 6792386
Fax 67900882
Pleasant hotel dating from the 18th century; it numbers Stendhal, Mazzini and Garibaldi among its past visitors. 51 rooms.

Columbus

(near St Peter's)
Via della Conciliazione 33, 00193
Tel. 6865435
Fax 6864874
Tastefully furnished hotel in a 15th-century palace built by Cardinal Domenico della Rovere. Original frescoes in the lobby, TV and mini-bar in the rooms. Close to the Vatican, the hotel is popular with visiting cardinals. 105 rooms.

Colosseum

(near Santa Maria Maggiore)
Via Sforza 10, 00184

. 4827228/4827078/4743486
ax 4827285
A comfortable hotel 10 minutes
from the Forum and the Colosseum. 45 rooms.

Condotti
(Corso/Piazza di Spagna)
Via Mario dei Fiori 37, 00187
Tel. 6794661/6790457
Quiet and comfortable hotel in
the heart of the shopping district.
19 rooms.

Dei Borgognoni
(Corso/Via del Tritone)
Via del Bufalo 126, 00187
Tel. 69941505
Fax 69941501
Elegant hotel offering excellent
service. Some of the 50 rooms
have a private garden or terrace.

Eden
(near Via Veneto)
Via Ludovisi 49, 00187
Tel. 4743551/4742401
Fax 4821584
Old-fashioned luxury hotel with
good views of the city from the
rooftop terrace restaurant. 116
rooms.

Edera
(near Colosseum)
Via Poliziano 75, 00184
Tel. 70453888/70453946

Fax 70453769
Quiet hotel with garden. No restaurant. 53 rooms.

Erdarelli
*(Piazza di Spagna/Largo del
Tritone)*
Via Due Macelli 28, 00187
Tel. 6791265/6784010
Fax 6790705
Unpretentious hotel in a very con-
venient location not far away from
the Spanish Steps. 28 comfortable
rooms.

Excelsior
(Via Veneto)
Via Veneto 125, 00197
Tel. 4708
Grand turn-of-the-century hotel,
recently renovated and extremely
comfortable. 329 rooms.

Fontana
(near Trevi Fountain)
Piazza di Trevi 96, 00187
Tel. 6786113/6790024
Comfortable hotel housed in a
converted monastery overlooking
the Trevi Fountain. Roof garden.
19 rooms.

Forum
(near Piazza Venezia)
Via Tor de' Conti 25, 00184
Tel. 6792446
Fax 6786479

Comfortable, elegantly furnished hotel with a spectacular view of the Imperial Forums from its delightful roof-garden restaurant. 76 rooms.

Gerber

(Prati)
Via degli Scipioni 241, 00192
Tel. 3221001/3219986
Fax 3217048
Small hotel in a quiet neighbourhood. A garden and sun terrace add to the comforts. 27 rooms.

Le Grand Hotel

(near Termini Station)
Via Vittorio Emanuele
Orlando 3, 00185
Tel. 4709
Fax 4823867
One of Rome's most sophisticated and well-established hotels, with monumentally proportioned salons, rooms and ornate decor. 171 rooms.

Gregoriana

(near the Spanish Steps)
Via Gregoriana 18, 00187
Tel. 6794269
Fax 6784258
A converted convent in a particularly pleasant location. Distinctive art-deco style and pretty, comfortable rooms add to the general pleasure. 19 rooms.

Hassler Villa Medici

(above the Spanish Steps)
Piazza Trinità dei Monti 6, 00187
Tel. 6782651
Fax 6789991
One of the world's most romantic locations in which to stay, right above the Spanish Steps, with furnishings, service and a spectacular Roman rooftop view to match. 101 rooms.

Holiday Inn Crowne Plaza Minerva

(Corso/Piazza Navona)
Piazza della Minerva 69, 00186
Tel. 69941888
Fax 6794165
A 17th-century *palazzo* that has been a lodging place since Napoleonic times, and is now Rome's newest luxury hotel. 134 rooms.

D'Inghilterra

(Corso/Piazza di Spagna)
Via Bocca di Leone 14, 00187
Tel. 69921366
Fax 69940828
An elegant hotel near the Spanish Steps. Antique furniture and a fine collection of Neapolitan gouaches preserve a distinct flavour of the past. Notable among former celebrity guests here are the writers Ernest Hemingway, Mark Twain and Henry James. 105 delightful rooms.

69

Locarno ▮▮
(near Piazza del Popolo)
Via della Penna 22, 00186
Tel. 3610841/3216030
Fax 3215249
Centrally located hotel with a charming vine-covered façade. 38 comfortable rooms.

Lord Byron ▮▮▮
Via Giuseppe De Notaris 5, 00197
Tel. 3220404/3224541
Fax 3220405
Elegant luxury hotel hosting one of Rome's most distinguished restaurants, Relais le Jardin. Garden. 50 rooms.

Margutta ▮
(Piazza del Popolo/Corso)
Via Laurina 34, 00187
Tel. 6798440
Small but centrally located hotel. Some of the rooms on the upper floor have their own terraces. 21 rooms.

Mediterraneo ▮▮▮
(near Termini Station)
Via Cavour 15, 00184
Tel. 4884051
Fax 4744105
A period piece from the 1930s in solemn classical style, with busts and statues, mosaics and maps on the theme of the Mediterranean.

Wonderful views from the 10th-floor terrace. 265 rooms.

Milani ▮▮
(near Termini Station)
Via Magenta 12, 00185
Tel. 4457051
Fax 4462317
On the more sedate side of Termini Station. Efficient service. 78 rooms.

Portoghesi ▮
(near Piazza Navona)
Via dei Portoghesi 1, 00186
Tel. 6864231
Fax 6876976
Comfortable, small hotel in a quiet corner of Rome's Centro Storico. Reasonably priced with air conditioning, television and telephones in each of the 27 rooms.

Quirinale ▮▮▮
(near Piazza della Repubblica)
Via Nazionale 7, 00184
Tel. 4707
Fax 4820099
Large hotel just next door to the charming Teatro dell'Opera. Garden. Outdoor dining in summer. 186 rooms.

Raphael ▮▮▮
(near Piazza Navona)
Largo Febo 2, 00186
Tel. 6508853/6508854

Fax 6878993
Vine-covered and intimate establishment, charmingly decorated with antiques in the lobby as well as the rooms. Restaurant and bar. 83 rooms.

Sant'Anselmo

(Aventine)
Piazza di Sant'Anselmo 2, 00153
Tel. 5743547
Fax 5783604
Very peaceful hotel with a pretty garden on the Aventine but not all that convenient for the centre of the city. 46 rooms.

Scalinata di Spagna

(above Piazza di Spagna)
Piazza Trinità dei Monti 17, 00187
Tel. 69940598
Fax 69940598
A fantastic view over the city and down the Spanish Steps from this charming small hotel. No restaurant. 15 rooms.

Del Senato

(near the Pantheon)
Piazza della Rotonda 73, 00186
Tel. 6793231/6784343
Fax 69940598
Comfortable hotel in the heart of the Centro Storico. Some rooms have view of the Pantheon. 51 rooms.

Sole

(near Campo de' Fiori)
Via del Biscione 76, 00186
Tel. 68806873/6879446
Fax 6893787
Budget-priced hotel in a convenient location. 58 rooms.

Sole Al Pantheon

(near the Pantheon)
Piazza della Rotonda 63, 00186
Tel. 6780441
Fax 6840689
An inn for 500 years, the hotel has recently been refurbished, retaining all its charm while adding modern comforts. Each of the 25 rooms is named after one of the illustrious guests of the past.

Suisse

(near Piazza di Spagna)
Via Gregoriana 56, 00187
Tel. 6783649
Fax 6781258
Comfortable, efficiently run hotel in a good location near the Spanish Steps. 28 rooms.

Villa Delle Rose

(near Termini Station)
Via Vicenza 5, 00185
Tel. 4451788
Fax 4451639
A former villa with a frescoed salon for a lounge, and a garden. Efficient and attractive. 37 rooms. **71**

Recommended Restaurants

Authentic Roman cuisine has its basis in *la cucina povera*, the cooking of the poor. You will therefore find simple but delicious traditional dishes in many a Roman *trattoria*, but also in the most elegant and expensive of restaurants. Below is a list of restaurants recommended by Berlitz; if you find other places worth recommending we'd be pleased to hear from you.

Note that after the *Ferragosto* festival (15 August) many restaurants close for two weeks as Romans head out of town.

The following symbols are designed to give you some idea of the price for a three-course meal with wine:

Ⅰ	below L35,000
Ⅱ	L35,000-70,000
Ⅲ	above L70,000

ROME

Andrea   Ⅲ
(near Via Veneto)
Via Sardegna 26, 00187
Tel. 4740557
Classic Italian cuisine in a classy setting. Excellent seafood dishes. Good wine list. Reservations are advised. Closed Sunday, Monday lunchtime and most of August.

Alberto Ciarla   Ⅲ
(Trastevere)
Piazza San Cosimato 40, 00153
Tel. (06) 5818668
The city's top restaurant for seafood, worth a visit for the fish tank. Outdoor dining. Dinner only. Reservations advised. Closed Sunday, 2 weeks in August and 2 weeks in December.

Apuleius   Ⅱ
(Aventine)
Via Tempio di Diana 15, 00153
Tel. 5742160/5746509
Fax 5746509
Quiet restaurant in a 1st-century Roman house serving seafood and hearty fare. A good mid-day stopping point for Aventine sightseers. Closed Sunday.

Artusiana   Ⅱ
(Trastevere)
Via della Penitenza 7, 00153
Tel. 68307053

A good place for risotto and pasta. Closed Sunday and Monday.

Il Bisticchiere

(near Piazza Navona)
Via dei Gigli d'Oro 2, 00186
Tel. 68308104
Fresh fish specialities although Chateaubriand on a splendid grill is to be recommended. Reservation advised. Open late.

Il Buco

(Corso/Pantheon)
Via di Sant'Ignazio 7, 00186
Tel. 6793298/6784467
Popular *trattoria* serving Tuscan specialities, with some dishes from Lazio as well. Closed Monday and 2 weeks in August.

La Campana

(near Piazza Navona)
Vicolo della Campana 18, 00186
Tel. 6875273/6867820
A popular local *trattoria* with all Italian favourites. Closed Monday and for the month of August.

Camponeschi

(Campo dei Fiori/Via Giulia)
Piazza Farnese 50, 00186
Tel. 6874927/6865244
Sophisticated menu and an elegant dining room with terrace view. Reservations advised. Open until late. Closed Sunday.

Cannavota

(St John Lateran)
Piazza di San Giovanni in Laterano 20, 00184
Tel. 77205007
Charming, easy-going *trattoria* with big portions. Good for lasagna, risotto and grilled fish. Closed Wednesday and for 3 weeks in August.

Casina Valadier

(above Piazza del Popolo)
Viale Belvedere al Pincio
Tel. 6792083
A romantic place with one of Rome's most splendid views, dominated by the great dome of St Peter's. Cuisine based on Italian regional cooking. Romans come here more for the atmosphere than the food. Reserve evenings and weekends. Closed Monday.

Checchino Dal 1887

(Testaccio)
Via di Monte Testaccio 30, 00153
Tel. 5743816
A legendary place, once the humblest of *trattorie* serving a cuisine based on the cheap cuts and offal from Testaccio's slaughterhouse. The presentation has been smartened up, but the tripe, brains and liver, sweetbreads and intestines are still the starting ingredients. Reservation essential for supper. **73**

...Sunday evening and all ...onday.

...ecco er Carrettiere ‖
(...rastevere)
Via Benedetta 10, 00153
Tel. 5800985
Colourful old Trastevere tavern offering Roman menu. Outdoor tables in summer. Reservation advised. Closed Sunday evening, all day Monday and in August.

Al Chianti ‖
(Porta Pia)
Via Ancona 17, 00198
Tel. 8551083/8416731
Serving Tuscan specialities. Reservations advised. Closed Sunday and in August.

Club 56 La Zeppa ‖
(Salario)
Via Basento 56, 00186
Tel. 85303349
A creative menu with dishes inspired by Greek and Italian cuisines. Reservations advised. Closed Sunday and in August.

Colline Emiliane ‖
(near Piazza Barberini)
Via degli Avignonesi 22, 00187
Tel. 4817538
Trattoria serving specialities from Emilia-Romagna. Reservation advised. Closed Friday and August.

74

Coriolano e Stefania ‖‖‖
(near Porta Pia)
Via Ancona 14, 00198
Tel. 8551122/8419501
An elegant place serving very nicely presented versions of hearty Roman fare and home-made pasta dishes. Reservations advised. Closed Sunday, weekends in July and in August.

Il Cortiletto ‖
(near Pantheon)
Piazza Capranica 77, 00186
Tel. 6793977
Charming restaurant offering traditional dishes such as risotto, *carpaccio* and many rich desserts. Closed Tuesday.

Crisciotti-al Boschetto ‖
(near Via Nazionale)
Via del Boschetto 30, 00184
Tel. 4744770
Rustic *trattoria* with delightful outdoor dining. Closed Saturday and August.

Il Drappo ‖
(Corso Vittorio Emanuele/Via Giulia)
Vicolo del Malpasso 9, 00186
Tel. 6877365
Small and attractive restaurant serving classic Sardinian dishes and wines. Reserve. Closed Sunday and for 2 weeks in August.

L'Eau Vive ▌▌

(near Largo Argentina)
Via Monterone 85, 00186
Tel. 68801095
Splendid French Colonial cuisine served in a restaurant run by French nuns and housed in a 16th-century papal palace. Advance reservations advised. Closed on Sunday and August.

Elettra ▌

(near Termini Station)
Via Principe Amedeo 72, 00185
Tel. 4745397
Popular local *trattoria* with traditional fare. Closed Saturday and for 3 weeks in August.

Les Etoiles ▌▌▌

(near Castel Sant'Angelo)
Via Vitelleschi 34, 00193
Tel. 6879558
Rooftop restaurant of the Hotel Atlante Star. Elegant food, plus a stunning view of St Peter's.

Da Fortunato ▌▌

(near Pantheon)
Via del Pantheon 55, 00186
Tel. 6792788
Trattoria serving regional specialities and seafood. Closed Sunday.

Da Giggetto ▌▌

Via del Portico d'Ottavia 21a,
00186 Tel. 6861105

One of the best-known addresses for traditional Roman specialities. Advance reservations are advised. Closed on Mondays and throughout July.

Giovanni ▌▌

(near via Veneto)
Via Marche 19
Tel. 4821834
Popular local restaurant serving good pasta dishes. Advance reservations are advised. Closed Friday evening, all day Saturday and for the month of August.

Al Girarrosto ▌▌
Toscano di Pietro Bruno

Via Germanico, 56
Tel. 39725717
Weell-situated restaurant near St Peter's. The principal specialities are Tuscan and Roman dishes. Particularly recommended for meat lovers.

Girone VI ▌▌

(near Largo Argentina)
Vicolo Sinibaldi 2, 00186
Tel. 68802831
The name means the Sixth Circle, a reference to the circle in *Dante's Inferno* devoted to gluttons. Culinary specialities from Provence and Liguria. Open evenings only. Reservations are advised. Closed Sunday.

Hassler Roof Garden ▌▌▌
(above Piazza di Spagna)
Piazza della Trinità dei Monti 6
Tel. 6792651
A restaurant at the top of the Hassler Hotel with a romantic view of the whole city. Excellent service and food. Reservations advised.

Insalata Ricca I ▌
(near Corso Vittorio Emanuele)
Largo dei Chiavari, 85
Tel. 68803656
Nice variety of fresh and savoury salads as well as succulent pasta dishes. No-smoking.

Margutta Vegetariano ▌▌
(near Piazza del Popolo)
Via Margutta 119
Tel. 6786033
Traditional vegetarian dishes from southern Italy served in pretty surroundings. Closed Sunday.

Mariano ▌▌
(near Via Veneto)
Via Piemonte 79, 00187
Tel. 4745256
Regional cheeses and home-style coking from the Marches. Reservation advised. Closed Sunday.

Da Mario ▌▌
(Corso/Piazza di Spagna)
Via della Vite 55, 00187
Tel. 6783818

Nicely cooked food from Tuscany with strong flavours, rich in meat and game and filling pasta dishes. Closed Sunday and August.

Il Matriciano ▌▌
(Prati)
Via dei Gracchi 55, 00192
Tel. 3212327
Close to the Vatican. Roman specialities served in a very comfortable atmosphere. Reservations advised. Closed on Wednesday from October to mid-June and on Saturday throughout the remainder of the year. Also closed for the month of August.

Al Moro ▌▌
(near Trevi Fountain)
Vicolo delle Bollette 13, between Via dei Crociferi and Via delle Muratte
Tel. 6783495
Busy, crowded place with excellent versions of salt cod and vegetable dishes. Reservation advised. Closed Sunday and for the month of August.

Nel Regno di Re Ferdinando ▌▌
(near Piazza Navona)
Via dei Banchi Nuovi 8
Tel. 68801167
Wonderful Neapolitan pasta dishes, seafood and pastries. Open

evenings only. Late-night dining. Closed Sunday and for 2 weeks in August.

L'Orso 80 ▥

(near Piazza Navona)
Via dell'Orso 33, 00186
Tel. 6864904/6861710
Uncomplicated meat and fish dishes cooked in the style of the Abruzzo, a friendly family-run restaurant. Closed Monday and for several weeks in August.

Papa Giovanni ▥▥

(near Piazza Navona)
Via dei Sediuri 4
Tel. 6865308
One of the city's top restaurants, where simple and classical dishes are prepared with style. The accent is on seasonal vegetables and fresh Lazio market produce. In addition there is good list of local wines.

Paris in Trastevere ▥

(Trastevere)
Piazza di San Callisto 7/a, 00153
Tel. 5815378
On offer at this delightful restaurant are a charming baroque dining room and a terrace for summer suppers. Closed Sunday evening, all day Monday and for the month of August.

La Pergola dell' Hotel Hilton ▥▥

(Monte Mario)
Via Cadlolo 101, 00136
Tel. 35091
In one of the city's finest restaurants, classical dishes are served by candlelight to a background accompaniment of soft piano music – all while you overlook the hills. Reservations essential. Closed Sunday. See p.67 for hotel (Cavalieri Hilton).

Al Piccolo Arancio ▯

(near Trevi Fountain)
Vicolo di Scanderberg 112
Tel. 6786139
In a narrow alley near the Trevi Fountain, this is an attractive little place which takes food seriously. Very good Roman specials and fish. Closed Monday and for the month of August.

Il Piccolo ▯

(near Piazza Navona)
Via del Governo Vecchio 74
Tel. 68801746
Lively and central wine bar with a buffet serving traditional fare.

Piperno ▥▥

(Jewish Ghetto)
Via Monte dei Cenci 9, 00186
Tel. 68802772

77

Expensive restaurant in the heart of the Ghetto serving Roman/Jewish specialities. Reservations advised. Closed Sunday evening and Monday.

Pizzeria Baffetto

(near Piazza Navona)
Via del Governo Vecchio 114
Tel. 6861617
A student hangout. The pizza is excellent. Closed Monday.

Pizzeria MonteCarlo

(near Corso Vittorio Emanuele)
Vicolo Savelli, 11/A - 13, 00186
Tel. 6861877
Excellent pizza. Student hangout.

Pizzeria Panattoni

(Trastevere)
Viale de Trastevere 53
Tel. 5800919
The pavement tables are always jammed with people enjoying good pizza and other Roman food.

Al Pompiere

(near Largo Argentina)
Via di Santa Maria dei Calderai 38
Tel. 6868377
Traditional Roman cooking prepared and served with great finesse in the heart of a busy quarter. Closed Sunday and mid-July to late August.

Porto di Ripetta

(Corso/Piazza del Popolo)
Via di Ripetta 250
Tel. 3612376
Seafood specialities. Original unfussy cooking. Reservations advised. Closed Sunday and for 15 days in August.

Relais la Piscine

(Parioli)
Via G Mangili 6, 00197.
Tel. 3223993
Creative cuisine with some Mediterranean and French inspiration and ingredients. Reservations advised. Closed Sunday evening.

Relais le Jardin

(Parioli)
Via Giuseppe De Notaris 5
Tel. 3224541
Exellent cuisine in the elegant restaurant of the Hotel Lord Byron (see p.xx). Reservations essential. Closed Sunday and for most of the month of August.

Le Restaurant del Grand Hotel

(near Termini Station)
Via V E Orlando 3
Tel. 4709
Sophisticated cuisine in the setting of the splendidly luxurious dining rooms of the Grand Hotel. Reservations essential.

Romolo a Porta Settimiana

(Trastevere)
Via di Porta Settimiana 8
Tel. 5818284
Classical Roman and also some very creative pasta dishes. Outdoor dining in the terraced garden in summer. Open late. Reservation advised. Closed Monday and for the month of August.

La Rosetta

(Corso/Piazza Navona)
Via della Rosetta 9
Tel. 68308841
Excellent seafood restaurant near the Pantheon. Reservations essential. Closed Sunday and August.

Sabatini

(Trastevere)
Vicolo di Santa Maria in Trastevere 18
Tel. 5818307
Seafood and Roman specialities. Closed Tuesday.

Sabatini a Santa Maria in Trastevere

(Trastevere)
Piazza di Santa Maria in Trastevere 13
Tel. 5812026
Sister restaurant to the Sabatini (above) also serving Roman specialities. Closed Wednesday.

Sans Souci

(near Via Veneto)
Via Sicilia 20
Tel. 4821814
Elegant restaurant offering a good range of international cuisine and traditional Roman dishes. Dinner only. Late-night suppers available. Reservations are advised. Closed on Mondays and for three weeks in August.

Taverna Flavia

(near Via XX Settembre)
Via Flavia 9
Tel. 4745214
Fashionable taverna open late. Closed for Saturday lunch and all day Sunday.

Taverna Giulia

(Corso Vittorio Emanuele/Tiber)
Vicolo dell'Oro 23
Tel. 6869768
Ligurian cuisine, much of it is green, the most famous of the dishes being *pesto* (basil sauce). Reservations are essential. Closed on Sundays and for the month of August.

Taverna Trevi

(Fontana di Trevi)
Via del Lavatore, 82
Tel. 6792470
An extensive menu offers many local specialities and service is **79**

...age of dishes available ... to budget.

...ativo di ...scrizione di un ...anchetto a Roma   ▯▯▯
(Trastevere)
Via della Luce 5
Tel. 5895234
Even the name is extravagant: 'Essay on a Roman banquet'. Splendid seafood in summer, game in winter. Reserve. Open evening only. Closed Sunday and for 3 weeks in August.

El Toulà   ▯▯▯
(Corso/Piazza Navona)
Via della Lupa 29/b.
Tel. 6873498/6873750
Elegant, popular restaurant near Piazza del Parliamento. Notable wine list. Reservations essential. Closed Saturday at lunch, all day Sunday and in August.

Vecchia Roma   ▯▯
(near Piazza Venezia)
Piazza di Campitelli 18.
Tel. 6864604
A lovely spot offering tables on the square in the summer and cosy dining rooms in the winter. A long list of dishes based on traditional, local ingredients. Reservations advised. Closed Wednesday and for 15 days in August.

LAZIO

Allo Sbarco di Enea   ▯▯
Via dei Romagnoli 675,
00119, Ostia Antica
Tel. (06) 5650034
The Roman equivalent of a theme restaurant, with mock-ancient frescoes, chariots, and waiters decked out in Roman costumes. Between the train station and the ruins. Closed Monday.

Bastianelli al Moro   ▯▯▯▯
Via Torre Clementina 312,
00054 Fiumicino
Tel. 6507210
Excellent restaurant specializing in seafood. Closed Monday and for the month of January.

Cecilia Metella   ▯▯
(Old Appian Way)
Via Appia Antica 125/127, 00179
Tel. 5136743
Pleasant restaurant with shady garden, sited near the ancient Roman tomb of Cecilia Metella. Closed Monday and in August.

Cacciani   ▯▯
Via Diaz 13, 00044 Frascati
Tel. (06) 9420378
Good cuisine, with outdoor dining on the terrace in summer. Closed Tuesday and for 2 weeks in January and mid-August.

Popes lived in the Lateran Palace for a thousand years until they moved to Avignon, and then to the Vatican in the 14th century. On a wooden table, incorporated in the high altar, St Peter himself is said to have celebrated mass.

Fire, earthquake and looting by the Vandals reduced the church to ruins over the centuries. The present basilica, little more than 300 years old, is at least the fifth on this site. But the bronze **central doors** go all the way back to ancient Rome, when they graced the entrance to the Curia in the Forum (see p.43). High above the basilica's façade, 15 giant white statues of Jesus, John the Baptist and Church sages stand out against the sky.

Transformed by Borromini in the 17th century, the interior of the church gives a predominant impression of sombre white and grey, more restrained than is usual for baroque architects. The only exuberant touches are the coloured marble inlays of the paving. In recesses along the nave stand several statues of the Apostles which were sculpted by pupils of Bernini.

The octagonal **baptistery** preserves some truly splendid 5th- and 7th-century mosaics. It was built over the baths of Constantine's second wife Fausta, where the first baptisms in Rome took place. The beautiful bronze doors of St John the Baptist's Chapel, removed from the Baths of Caracalla (see p.50), sing musically on their hinges when they are opened.

Foremost exponents of the cosmatesque style of inlaid marble, the brothers Jacopo and Pietro Vassalletto have excelled themselves in the **cloisters**, where alternating straight and twisted columns, set in mosaic-style, create a perfect setting for meditation.

An ancient edifice opposite the basilica – almost all that's left of the old Lateran Palace – shelters the **Scala Santa**, the holy stairway brought back by St Helena from Jerusalem and said to have been trodden by Jesus in the house of Pontius Pilate. The devout climb the 28 marble steps on their knees. **81**

Outside the basilica stands an Egyptian **obelisk** brought from the Temple of Ammon in Thebes. It's the tallest in the world – 31m (102ft) – and the oldest (1449 BC) of the 13 still standing in Rome.

ST PAUL'S OUTSIDE THE WALLS

St Paul's Basilica, the largest in Rome after St Peter's, was built by Constantine in AD 314 and enlarged by Valentinian II and Theodosius. Astonishingly, it survived intact until destroyed by fire in 1823. Today, a faithful restoration, though preserving only a little of its former splendour, has recreated San Paolo fuori le Mura's original form.

A **tabernacle**, designed by the 13th-century sculptor Arnolfo di Cambio and retrieved from the ashes of the great fire, decorates the high altar under which lies the burial place of St Paul. After Paul was beheaded, a Roman matron, Lucina, placed the body here in her family vault. Constantine later encased it in a sarcophagus of marble and bronze, which was looted by Saracen invaders in AD 846.

Above the 86 Venetian marble columns runs a row of mosaic medallions representing all the popes from St Peter to the present day. Pause in the peaceful Benedictine **cloister**, designed by Pietro Vassalletto and surpassing even his work at St John Lateran. Slender, spiralled columns in the cosmatesque tradition glitter with green, red and gold mosaic, enclosing a garden of roses and gently rippling fountain.

SAN CLEMENTE

This gem of a church hides a fascinating history which can be traced down through each of its three levels. The present church, dating to the 12th century, is built in basilica form with three naves divided by ancient columns and embellished by a pavement of geometric designs. A symbolic mosaic in the apse features the Cross as the Tree of Life nourishing all living things – birds, animals and plants.

To the right of the nave, a staircase leads down to the **4th-century basilica**, which underpins the present church. The Romanesque frescoes, unfortunately, have now drastically faded, but copies show how they were in near-perfect condition when they were uncovered earlier this century.

An ancient stairway leads further underground to a maze of corridors and chambers, believed to be the home of St Clement himself, third successor to St Peter as Pope. Also down here is the earliest religious structure on this site, a pagan **temple** (*Mithraeum*) dedicated to the god Mithras. A sculpture shows the Persian god of light slaying a bull. The sound of trickling water from a nearby stream echoes eerily through these subterranean chambers as it drains off into the Cloaca Maxima (see p.40).

SANTA PRASSEDE

Though unremarkable from the outside, this little church is enchanting in the intimacy of its interior. St Praxedes and her sister Pudentiana we daughters of a Roman ser who as one of the first conve to Christianity gave shelter t St Peter.

Delicate 9th-century mosaics of Jesus and four angels glittering with gold cover the **Chapel of St Zeno**, making it the city's most important Byzantine monument. It was designed as a tomb for Theodora, mother of Pope Paschal I – mediaeval Romans called it the 'Garden of Paradise' because of its beauty. To the right is a fragment of rare jasper, said to have come from the column to which Jesus was tied for his flagellation.

SAN PIETRO IN VINCOLI

St Peter in Chains may not attract a second glance (and might even prefer it that way, given the hordes of visitors) if it didn't contain one of Michelangelo's greatest sculptures, his formidable **Moses**. Intended for St Peter's as part of Michelangelo's unsuccessful project for Julius II's tomb, **83**

...ue of the great biblical ... sits in awesome majesty ...e centre of the monument. ...ou can imagine how grandiose the original plan must have been when you realize from his sideward stare that Moses was supposed to be just a corner figure facing the centre. The horns on his head continue the traditional mediaeval mistranslation of the Hebrew for halo-like rays of light. On each side, the comparatively passive figures of Jacob's two wives, a prayerful Rachel and melancholy Leah, were the last completed sculptures of Michelangelo.

Empress Eudoxia founded the church in the 5th century, on the site of the Roman law court where St Peter was tried and sentenced. It was built as a sanctuary for the chains with which Herod bound St Peter in Palestine together with those used when he was imprisoned in Rome. They are kept in a bronze reliquary beneath the high altar.

THE GESÙ

Severe and relatively discreet on its own piazza west of the Piazza Venezia, the Gesù is the mother church of the Jesuits and was a major element in their Counter-Reformation campaign. Begun as their Roman headquarters in 1568, its open plan became the model for the congregational churches that were to regain popular support from the Protestants. While its façade is more sober than the baroque churches put up as the movement gained

Impressive holy-life includes the extravagant ceiling fresco in San Pietro in Vincoli (left) and the soaring dome of the Gesù (right).

momentum, the **interior** glorifies the newly-found militancy in gleaming bronze, gold, marble and precious stones.

St Ignatius Loyola, a Spanish soldier who founded the order, has a fittingly magnificent **tomb** under a richly decorated altar in the left transept, with a profusion of lapis lazuli. The globe at the top is said to be the largest piece of this stone in the world.

SANT'IGNAZIO

In gentler contrast, the church of Sant'Ignazio stands in an enchanting stage-set of russet and ochre rococo houses. Inside, Andrea Pozzo (himself a Jesuit priest and designer of the saint's tomb in the Gesù) has painted a superb *trompe-l'oeil* **ceiling fresco** (1685) depicting St Ignatius's entry into paradise. Stand on a buff stone disk in the nave's central aisle and you will have the extraordinary impression of the whole building rising above you through the ingenious architectural effect of the painting. From any other point, the columns appear to collapse. From another disk further up the aisle you can admire the celestial dome above the high altar, but as you advance, it begins to take on strange proportions – just another illusionist painting.

ums

Romans have been enthu-
siastic patrons and collectors
of art for millennia and their
museums are packed with treasures. It would take a lifetime
to explore them all, but here
are a few of the best.

GALLERIA BORGHESE

The avid and ruthless art
collector Cardinal Scipione
Borghese conceived this hand-
some baroque villa in the Villa
Borghese (see p.31) as a home
for his small but outstanding
collection, using his prestige
as the nephew of Pope Paul V
to extort coveted masterpieces
from their owners.

The gallery has been undergoing extensive restoration for
several years, during which
time only a part of the collection has been on view. A recent development has seen the
works of art removed for an
indeterminate period to the

Palazzo San Michele in Via di San Michele in Trastevere. It is advisable to check with the Tourist Office (see p.140) before you make a special trip.

The highlights of the collection are several astonishing **sculptures** by the cardinal's young protégé, Bernini. These include busts of his patron; a vigorous *David* (said to be a youthful self-portrait); and a graceful sculpture, *Apollo and Daphne*, in which the water-nymph turns into a laurel just as the god is about to seize her. In a later addition, and now the star attraction, Antonio Canova portrays Napoleon's sister Pauline, who married into the Borghese family, as a naked reclining Venus.

There are some exceptional **paintings** in the collection, including Raphael's *Descent from the Cross*, Titian's *Sacred and Profane Love*, Caravag-

gio's *David with the Head of Goliath* and *Madonna of the Serpent*, along with works by Botticelli, Rubens, Dürer and Cranach.

VILLA GIULIA

This pleasure palace of a pope, dating from the 16th century and north west of the Villa Borghese, is now the lovely setting for Italy's finest museum of **Etruscan art**. Although much of this pre-Roman civilization is still a mystery, the Etruscans left a wealth of detail about their customs and everyday life by burying the personal possessions of the dead with them in their tombs.

Replicas show the round, stone burial mounds, built like huts. Room after room is filled with objects from the tombs: bronze statues of warriors in battledress; shields, weapons and chariots (even the skeletons of two horses); gold, silver jewellery, decorative vases imported by Etruscans from Greece; and a host of everyday cooking utensils, mirrors and combs. Note the bronze toilet **87**

Canova's seductive statue of Napoleon's femme fatale sister, Pauline Borghese, gets top billing at the Galleria Borghese.

box adorned with figures of the Argonauts. The highlight is a life-size terracotta sculpture, for a sarcophagus lid, of a blissful young couple reclining on a banquet couch.

MUSEO NAZIONALE ROMANO

You'll find the best introduction to Rome's Greek and Roman antiquities in this superb collection housed in the Roman Baths of Diocletian. Larger even than those of Caracalla, Diocletian's baths covered 120ha (300 acres), part of which are now occupied by the Piazza della Repubblica and Michelangelo's church of Santa Maria degli Angeli, near Termini Station.

The *piccolo chiostro* (small cloister) of the old Carthusian monastery provides an attractive setting for the magnificent **Ludovisi Collection**, assembled by Cardinal Ludovico Ludovisi in the 17th century. Among the most important pieces, look out for the marble altar-top known as the *Ludovisi Throne*, an original Greek work from the 5th century BC, with exquisitely carved reliefs of Aphrodite and a maiden playing the flute. Also seek out the tragic statue of a Barbarian warrior in the act of killing himself and his wife rather than submit to slavery.

Other highlights include the *Apollo of the Tiber*, a copy of a bronze group by the young Pheidias; a copy, probably the best ever, of Myron's famed *Discobolos* (Discus-Thrower); the *Daughter of Niobe*, an original from the 5th century BC; the *Venus of Cyrene*; a bronze of a young man leaning on a lance; and a variety of portrait sculptures, including one of Emperor Augustus.

The **landscape frescoes** taken from the Imperial Villa of Livia show nature at its most bountiful, with flowers, trees, birds and fruit painted with great attention to detail.

Sadly, only a limited number of rooms in the museum have been open to the public in recent years, although there are plans to house some of the collection in the nearby Palazzo Massimo.

GALLERIA NAZIONALE D'ARTE ANTICA

The Palazzo Barberini (on the Via delle Quattro Fontane) provided another architectural battleground for rivals Borromini and Bernini, each of whom built one of its grand staircases and contributed to the superb façade. It is worth a visit as much for its baroque décor as for its collection of paintings. Art and architecture come together in the palace's **Great Hall**, with Pietro da Cortona's dazzling illusionist ceiling fresco, *Triumph of Divine Providence*.

Most of the national art collection is hung in the first-floor gallery (the rest is housed in the Palazzo Corsini across the Tiber in Trastevere). Works include a Fra Angelico triptych, the famous portrait of King Henry VIII by Hans Holbein, and paintings by Titian, Tintoretto, and El Greco. Look for Raphael's *La Fornarina*, said to be a portrait of his mistress, and Caravaggio's depiction of Judith in the act of severing the head of Holofernes.

GALLERIA DORIA PAMPHILI

The vast Palazzo Doria in the Corso is still the private residence of the Doria family, but the public are allowed in several days a week to view their rich collection of paintings, assembled over hundreds of years. You can't do without a catalogue, as the paintings are identifiable only by number.

Much of the collection is poorly lit, but there are a number of masterpieces from the 15th-17th centuries, including works by Titian, Veronese, Raphael and Caravaggio, as well as from the Dutch and Flemish schools. Look out for the evocative landscape of the *Flight into Egypt* by Annibale Carracci and the windswept *Naval Battle in the Bay of Naples* by Breughal the Elder.

You'll find a nice stylistic contrast in a little room off the galleries, which juxtaposes a brilliant worldly portrait by Velázquez of Innocent X, the Pamphili family pope, alongside a more serene marble bust of him by Bernini. **89**

Excursions

The main excursions into the Lazio, or Latium, countryside around Rome today are those that ancient Romans took to holiday homes by the sea or nearby hills and lakes. Before any of these, however, you should take an important short trip just outside the city walls to the Old Appian Way.

OLD APPIAN WAY

Heading south east through the Porta San Sebastiano, look back for a good view of the old **Aurelian Wall**, still enclosing part of Rome. Its massive defensive ramparts stretch into the distance, topped by towers and bastions built to resist the onslaught of Barbarian invasions in the 3rd century.

Ahead lies a narrow lane, hemmed in at first by hedges and the high walls of film stars' and millionaires' homes – the **Old Appian Way**. When Appius Claudius the Censor opened it and gave it his name in 312 BC, this was the grandest road the Western world had

ever known. You can still see some of the original paving stones over which the Roman legions marched on their way to Brindisi to set sail for the Levant and North Africa.

Since by law burials could not take place within the city walls, the tombs of the dead were built along this road. On either side lie the ruins of sepulchres of 20 generations of patrician families, some with simple tablets, others with impressive mausoleums. For the same reason, the Christians built their cemeteries in the catacombs here.

At a fork in the road, the chapel of **Domine Quo Vadis** marks the spot where St Peter, fleeing Nero's persecution in Rome, is said to have encountered Christ and asked: '*Domine, quo vadis?*' ('Whither goest thou, Lord?'). Christ is believed to have replied: 'I go to Rome to be crucified again.' Ashamed of his fear, Peter turned back to Rome and his own crucifixion. The little chapel contains a copy of a stone with a footprint said to have been left by Christ (the original is in the Basilica of San Sebastiano).

Further along the Appia Antica, within a short distance of each other, are three of Rome's most celebrated catacombs: St Callixtus, Domitilla and St Sebastian. About six million early Christians, among them many martyrs and saints, were buried in 50 of these vast cemeteries. Knowledgeable guides accompany you in groups into a labyrinth of smelling tunnels burrowed into the s tufa rock, sometimes deep (claustrophobes abstain). Paintings and c ings adorn the catacombs w precious examples of early Christian art.

The entrance to the **Catacombs of St Calixtus** lies at the end of an avenue of cypresses. An official tour takes

---

The Third City

The historic centre of Rome has been kept mercifully free of antagonistic 20th-century innovations. But there is an ultramodern 'Third Rome', 5km (3 miles) south along the Ostian Way, which was Mussolini's dream, intended to rival the glories of the Imperial and Renaissance cities.

Known simply by its initials EUR (pronounced 'Ay-oor'), this complex of massive white marble buildings, with wide avenues and open spaces grouped around an artificial lake, was designed for a world fair in 1942 to mark 20 years of Fascism. The war interrupted construction, however, and the fair never took place.

In recent years, EUR has developed into a thriving township of government ministries, offices, conference centres and fashionable apartments. Several buildings remain from Mussolini's time, including the formidable cube of arches of the *Palazzo della Civiltà del Lavoro* (Palace of Workers), known as the 'Square Colosseum'. For the 1960 Olympics, architect Pier Luigi Nervi designed the huge, domed Palazzo dello Sport.

second level , where you will ...ial niches, called ... into the rock one ...e other on either side ...e dark galleries. Occasionally the narrow passages open out into larger chambers or *cubicula*, where a family would be buried together. One such crypt sheltered the remains of 3rd-century popes; another held the body of St Cecilia until it was transferred to the church of Santa Cecilia in Trastevere (the statue of the saint lying in a recess is a copy of the one by Stefano Maderno in the church, see p.41).

In the **Catacombs of St Sebastian**, the bodies of the Apostles Peter and Paul are said to have been hidden for several years during the 3rd-century persecutions. You can still see graffiti in Latin and Greek invoking the two saints.

The **tomb of Cecilia Metella** dominates the Appian landscape. This almost unknown noblewoman was a relative of the immensely rich Crassus who financed Julius Caesar's early campaigns. A 14th-century Roman family added the castellated parapet when they turned it into a fortress.

Alongside extends the well-preserved **Circus of Maxentius**, built for chariot races in AD 309 under the last pagan emperor, who carried out the final wave of Christian persecutions in Rome.

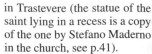

A spectacular display from the fountains of the Villa d'Este.

Turn off the Via Appia to visit the **Fosse Ardeatine**, a place of pilgrimage for modern Italians. In March 1944, in retaliation for the killing of 32 German soldiers by the Italian Resistance, the Nazis rounded up at random 335 Italian men (10 for each German and an extra 15 for good measure) and machine-gunned them in the sandpits of the Via Ardeatina. Once the Germans left Rome, a poignant memorial was raised here to the dead, among them a boy of 14 years.

TIVOLI

The picturesque town of Tivoli perches on a steep slope amid the woods, streams and twisted silvery olive trees of the Sabine Hills. Inhabited even in ancient times, when it was known as *Tibur*, Tivoli prospered throughout the Middle Ages and thus preserves interesting Roman remains as well as mediaeval churches, and the Renaissance villa and gardens.

Trains leave Stazione Termini every 15 minutes for Rebibbia terminal (metro line B).

Buses make the connection from here to Tivoli. By car the drive takes 1¼-hour (30km/19 miles) along the old Roman chariot road (since repaved!) of the Via Tiburtina.

The **Villa d'Este** sprawls along the hillside. From its balconies you can look down on the gardens, which fall away in a series of terraces – a paradise of dark cypresses, fountains (estimated at 500), grottoes, pools and statues.

Cardinal Ippolito II d'Este conceived this pleasure garden in the 16th century and the architect Pirro Ligorio, with that genius for playing with water that has characterized the Romans since ancient times, created it. On the **Terrace of 100 Fountains** water-jets splash into a long basin guarded by statues of eagles. The **Organ Fountain**, originally accompanied by organ music, cascades steeply down the rocks. On the lowest level three large deep pools contrast in their stillness with the rush and roar of water elsewhere. The architect took particular delight in strange fantasies, such as the **93** rows of sphinxes who spurt water from their nipples, or hidden jets which sprayed the unsuspecting passer-by. Don't worry, though – you won't be in for any unpleasant shocks – the water tricks are no more.

 Tucked away at the foot of the hills lie the haunting ruins of **Villa Adriana** (Hadrian's Villa). Spread over 70ha (173 acres), this retirement hide-away of the great emperor-builder (the Pantheon, see p. 36, and Hadrian's Wall in Britain are among his achieve-ments) was designed to recap-ture some of the architectural marvels of his empire, espe-cially Greece, which he loved above all else. These travel memoirs for his old age were filled with treasures that have since found their way to mu-seums around the world.

Those arriving at the villa by public bus are dropped off at the main gate and ticket of-fice. Tourist coaches and pri-vate cars continue up the drive to the car-park in the grounds. An excellent scale model here will give you an overview of the whole. As you will see,

94

this was more a miniature city than a villa. The monumental baths, separate Greek and Lat-in libraries, temples and pavil-ions together make up the home of a man who drew no distinction between the plea-sures of mind and body.

You enter the ruins through the colonnades of the Greek-style **Stoa Poikile** (Painted Portico), which leads to the main Imperial residence. Ad-joining the palace are guest rooms, their black and white mosaic floors still visible, and an underground passageway in which the servants moved about unseen.

The enchanting **Villa dell' Isola**, a pavilion surrounded by a little reflecting pool and circular portico, epitomizes all the magic of the place. To the south, remnants of arches and copies of Greek-style caryatids (female statues used as pillars) surround the **Pool of Cano-pus** leading to the sanctuary of the Egyptian god Serapis. Barbarians and museum cura-tors have removed most of the villa's treasures, but a stroll among the remaining pillars, arches and mosaics in gardens running wild among the olive trees, cypresses and umbrella pines can be marvellously evocative of a lost world.

OSTIA ANTICA

Excavations continue to uncover fascinating sections of what was once the seaport and naval base of ancient Rome. The long-buried city of Ostia stands at the mouth (*ostium*) of the Tiber, 23km (14 miles) south west of the capital on the shores of the Tyrrhenian Sea.

Sea-going vessels were unable to travel inland along the shallow Tiber, so river barges plied back and forth from the port, carrying Rome's supply of food and building materials. During its heyday, Ostia had 100,000 residents and boasted splendid baths, a theatre, temples and imposing houses.

Ostia's well-preserved ruins are set among cypresses and pines and reveal more about daily life and the building methods of ancient Rome than do those of the capital. Excavations since the 19th century

have unearthed warehouses, apartments known as *insulae* (islands), and private houses facing out to sea and decorated with mosaics and murals.

The **Piazzale delle Corporazioni** (Square of the Corporations) housed 70 commercial offices round a porticoed central temple to Ceres, goddess of agriculture. Mosaic mottoes and emblems in the pavement tell of the trading of grain factors, caulkers, ropemakers and shipowners from all over the world. The **theatre** next door was built by Agrippa. It is worth the climb up the tiered seats for a view over the whole ruined city.

As in Rome, the **Forum** was the focus of city life, dominated at one end by the Capitol, a temple dedicated to Jupiter, Juno and Minerva, and at the other by the Temple of Rome and Augustus, with the Curia (seat of the municipal authorities) and the basilica, or law courts, lying between.

To see a typical residence, visit the **House of Cupid and Psyche**, with its rooms paved in marble built round a central **95** garden courtyard. Nearby a small **museum** traces Ostia's history through statues, busts and frescoes.

The modern seaside resort of Lido di Ostia attracts week-ending Romans, who flock to the grey-sand beaches. Swimming is not recommended because of pollution. To make up for this, dine in one of the cheerful open-air restaurants.

THE ALBAN HILLS AND CASTEL GANDOLFO

Immediately to the south east of Rome, the scattered hill-towns known as the *Castelli Romani* (Roman Castles) began as fortified refuges during mediaeval civil wars. Today, it is just the summer heat that drives Romans out on daytrips to the vineyards here.

The Pope's official summer home is at **Castel Gandolfo**, above Lake Albano, where he relaxes in the huge palace designed by Carlo Maderno, set in beautiful landscaped gardens. On Wednesdays the pope no longer holds audience here, but flies by helicopter to the

96

Vatican for his usual appearance. The palace, gardens and Vatican Observatory in the grounds are closed to visitors. A terrace near the papal palace looks down on the deep, dark blue waters of **Lake Albano**, lying in an old forested volcanic crater below.

The towns of Frascati, Grottaferrata, Marino and Rocca di Papa make delightful stops, not least for a cool glass of their estimable white wine (especially during the autumn grape-harvests).

CERVETERI

If the Villa Guilia in Rome (see p.87) and the Gregorian-Etruscan Museum in the Vatican (see p.58) have aroused your curiosity about the Etruscans, it is worth making a trip to the ancient **necropolis** at Cerveteri, 43km (27 miles) north west of Rome. Known in ancient times as *Caere*, it was one of the original 12 towns of the powerful Etruscan League, though it declined in the 3rd century BC after becoming a Roman dependency.

The scores of **tombs** here represent every kind of burial from the early shaft and pit graves to *tumuli*, dating from the 7th-1st centuries BC. Stucco decorations and rock carvings represent the weapons, domestic animals and even household pots and pans that Etruscans felt they would need in the after-life. Most famous is the **Regolini-Galassi tomb**, whose riches are in the Gregorian-Etruscan Museum.

Unfortunately, many tombs have been plundered by graverobbers – a destruction which continues today. However, the **Museo Nazionale di Cerveteri**, in a 16th-century castle, displays chronologically a rich collection of objects from the tombs, including sarcophagi, sculptures and wall paintings.

Castel Gandolfo, high up in the Alban Hills, overlooks the dark blue waters of Lake Albano and houses the summer retreat of the Pope.

What to Do

Entertainment

Rome offers a host of evening entertainments, particularly in the summer months when the balmy evenings entice everyone outdoors. You can choose from the hottest of discos and nightclubs to the coolest of classical music, not to mention lively street festivals full of dancing, fireworks and open-air dining. Rome's popular summer festival, *L'Estate Romana*, runs from June to September and offers music, film, dance and theatre in venues across the city, many of them open air.

Concerts of **classical music** are performed in a number of picturesque and historic

*R*ome's caribinieri *blow their own trumpets on the Scalinata della Trinità dei Monti – the famous Spanish Steps.*

settings, including the Campidoglio (see p.25), the Isola Tiberina (see p.39) and the cloister of Santa Maria della Pace. The ruins of the Baths of Caracalla (see p.50) are the spectacular location for a summer season of **opera and ballet**. Military and civilian bands perform free concerts in the Pincio gardens (see p.30) from late April to mid-July. **Music clubs** also abound in Rome, with all kinds of music ranging from jazz, blues and folk to rock, reggae and salsa.

Cinemas will usually dub foreign-language films into Italian. An exception is the Pasquino in Trastevere, which screens recent American and British movies with the original soundtrack.

For up-to-the-minute information about what's going on in Rome, consult the entertainment supplement *Trovaroma* in the Thursday edition of *La Repubblica* newspaper. The Rome Tourist Board (see p.140) provides a monthly guide to events in the city and its surroundings: the *Carnet di Roma*.

CALENDAR OF EVENTS

January
5-6 Jan – *Befana* (Epiphany) – Festival on Piazza Navona.

February/March
Carnival – Period preceding Lent marked by masked processions and parades.

March
9 Mar – *Festa di San Francesco Romana* – at Piazzale del Colosseo for blessing.

March-April
Good Friday – the Pope leads the Procession of the Cross at 9pm from the candlelit Colosseum to the Forum.
Easter Sunday – the Pope blesses the crowds from the balcony of St Peter's at noon.

April-May
Festa della Primavera (Spring Festival) – the Spanish Steps flow with pink azaleas.
21 April – Rome's founding. International Horse Show in the Villa Borghese Park.
Tennis championships in the Foro Italico.

99

June
Festa della Repubblica – military parade along Via dei Fori Imperiali.
29 June – *Festa di San Pietro e San Paolo* – solemn rites in St Peter's Square.

July
Noiantri festival in Trastevere.

August
5 Aug – *Festa della Madonna della Neve* in Santa Maria Maggiore.
15 Aug – *Ferragosto* or Feast of the Assumption.

September
Open-air art exhibition in Via Margutta.

December
Cultural Heritage Week – free admission to state museums and monuments (first week).
Children's toy fair on Piazza Navona (until 6 Jan).
8 December – *Festa della Madonna Immacolata* (Immaculate Conception).
24 December – the Pope celebrates midnight mass at St Peter's Basilica.

Shopping

Italy's great visual culture combining a long artisan tradition and modern design flair come together to make shopping in Rome a delight. You won't necessarily find bargain-basement prices, but you will get superb quality and excellent service.

WHERE TO SHOP

The most fashionable shopping district in Rome lies between Piazza di Spagna and Via del Corso. The best in high fashion, jewellery, silk and leather is to be found in the elegant shops of Via Condotti and neighbouring streets such as Via Borgognona, Via Frattina and Via Bocca di Leone.

Via Cola di Rienzo, on the right bank of the River Tiber, not far from the Vatican, is a less exclusive shopping street, but its stores offer excellent quality. Via Nazionale, Via del Tritone and Via del Corso are less expensive places to shop for both fashionable clothes and leather.

Specialist shops which are often family-run and generations old are the rule in Rome. You won't find here the grand department stores boasted by other capital cities. The best of Rome's few big stores are Coin (Piazzale Appio, near St John Lateran) and La Rinascente (main branch at Piazza Colonna). More downmarket alternatives are the Standa and Upim chains, with branches throughout the city. All these have the advantage of longer opening hours than some of the smaller shops.

Be prepared to haggle if you go to Porta Portese, Rome's famous **flea market** held on Sunday morning in the streets and alleys running beside Via Portuense in Trastevere. Here you will find new and old

Rome's celebrated antiques shops depend on the painstaking craft skills of their restorers.

clothes, antique bric-à-brac, furniture, jewellery and books, but also the odd pickpocket, so take care.

The large **outdoor market** in Via Sannio (near St John Lateran) is good for bargain clothes. Piazza Vittorio Emanuele II (near Santa Maria Maggiore) has a colourful food market as well as stalls selling clothes and fabrics.

WHAT TO BUY

Antiques: it's no surpise to find antique dealers by the score in a city 2,700 years old. Rome's dealers sell exquisite (but expensive) silver, glass, porcelain, furniture and paintings. The best antiques shops are in Via del Babuino and Via Margutta (between the Spanish Steps and the Piazza del Popolo), Via Giulia (behind Palazzo Farnese) and Via dei Coronari, historically known as the Street of the Rosary Makers (near Piazza Navona).

Only buy antiques or art works from a reputable dealer, who will provide a certificate of guarantee and obtain the necessary government permit for export.

Books and prints: the market at Largo Fontanella di Borghese (off Via del Corso) specializes in original and reproduction prints and books.

Ceramics: colourful, attractively designed carafes, jugs, plates, bowls and tiles are available. Myricae in Via Frattina is good for reasonably priced regional handicrafts.

Fashion: Rome is second to none when it comes to stylish high-fashion clothes. All the big names of Italian *alta moda* are represented in the Piazza di Spagna area. Look out for Giorgio Armani, Fendi, Valentino, and Krizia.

You'll also find elegantly tailored men's clothes, both custom-made and ready-to-wear. La Cicogna, which has branches throughout the city, provides beautiful clothes for children.

Food and wine: good gastronomic delicacies to take home

with you include cheese (fresh Parmesan), salami, the Parma and San Daniele ham (*prosciutto crudo*), 'extra virgin' olive oil, wines from the Castelli Romani and fiery *grappa*.

Ai Monasteri in Piazza delle Cinque Lune (near Piazza Navona) sells liqueurs, confectionery, olive oil, honey and other products made by Italian monks.

Jewellery: you'll find fine antique jewellery in Rome, as well as modern designs and costume jewellery. For sheer opulence, nothing can quite match the elegant premises of Bulgari in Via Condotti.

Leather: stylish leather goods – shoes, handbags, wallets, luggage and gloves – abound. You'll find Ferragamo and Campanile in Via Condotti.

Textiles: beautiful silks, colourful knitwear and hand-embroidered table linen supplied by Rome's shops. Cesari sells luxurious furnishing fabrics in Via del Babuino and linens in Via Barberini.

High fashion or alta moda with grand designer names can be completely free when you go window-shopping in Rome.

Eating Out

Do as the Romans do with great enthusiasm and turn your eating out into an evening out. They like to spend hours over a leisurely meal of innumerable courses in the genial company of friends in one of the *trattorie* or restaurants which abound in the city. Now that traffic has been banned from large sections of Rome's historic centre, outdoor dining on balmy summer evenings can once more be a delight.

Choice spots are Trastevere (see p.41), which boasts scores of little *trattorie*, and the Jewish Ghetto (see p.38), with its own specialities. You should also take time to drive out at least once into the countryside beyond the walls to lunch or dine in one of the restaurants

*F*or a juicy, traditional slice of pizza in a mind-blowing range of varieties, just about anywhere in Rome can be recommended.

along the Via Appia Antica or the roads to the Alban Hills (see p.96) or Ostia (see p.95).

WHERE TO EAT

Only in hotels catering to tourists will you find an English or American-style breakfast. Otherwise go to a good *caffè* on the piazza and settle happily for the *prima colazione* of superb coffee, *espresso* (black) or *cappuccino* (with foaming hot milk), accompanied by a delicious sweet *cornetto* (croissant).

For a quick snack at lunchtime, choose a *tavola calda*, a stand-up bar serving a variety of hot and cold dishes throughout the day, to take away or eat on the spot. You can also have delicious sandwiches made up for you at a local delicatessen (*pizzichieria*). Ask for *panino ripieno*, a bread roll filled with whichever sausage, cheese or salad you choose from the inviting display on the counter.

Fast-food restaurants have been springing up all over Rome in the last few years. The last straw came for many

gourmets when the first MacDonald's in Italy opened in Rome in 1986. More and more ethnic eating places have also been appearing in the city. Chinese restaurants are particularly noticeable, but you can also try African, Arab, Greek, Indian, Japanese, Lebanese and Mexican cuisines. Vegetarian restaurants are still thin on the ground, but gaining in popularity.

In theory, a *ristorante* is usually a larger and more elaborate establishment than a family-style *trattoria* or rustic *osteria*. But in Rome the distinction is blurred beyond all recognition, thus one of the grandest and priciest restaurants in the city may call itself a humble *osteria*.

The price should not be taken as an indication of the quality of the cuisine; an expensive restaurant may offer a superb meal with service to match, but you may also be paying for the location. Only a few steps away from such famous tourist spots as the Piazza del Popolo and Piazza Navona, you'll find numerous **105**

*T*he Pantheon provides a timeless backdrop for eating out in
the Piazza della Rotonda.

trattorie, with lower prices, where the ambience, such an important aspect of an Italian meal, is much more appealing and the food has real character.

Restaurants are obliged to display the menu with prices in the window or just inside the door, so you will have an idea of what's on offer before you take the plunge.

WHEN TO EAT

Roman restaurants serve lunch from 12.30 to 3pm and dinner from 8 to 11pm. Some offer late-night supper and are open until 1, 2 or 3am. Each restaurant is closed one day a week, which will vary. If you are set on a particular venue, it is advisable to book by telephone, especially during peak hours (around 1.30pm and 9pm).

WHAT TO EAT

Antipasti: any *trattoria* worth its olive oil will set out on a long table near to the entrance a truly artistic display of its antipasti (*hors d'oeuvre*). The best way to get to know the delicacies is to make up your own assortment (*antipasto misto*). Both attractive to look at and tasty are the cold *peperoni*: red, yellow and green peppers grilled, skinned and then marinated in olive oil and a little lemon juice.

Mushrooms (*funghi*), courgettes (*zucchini*), aubergines (*melanzane*), artichokes (*carciofi*) and fennel (*finocchio*) also come cold, with a dressing (*pinzimonio*). One of the most refreshing antipasti is *mozzarella alla caprese*, slices of soft *mozzarella* cheese and tomato in a dressing of fresh basil and olive oil. Ham from Parma or San Daniele is paper thin, served with melon (*prosciutto con melone*) or, even better, fresh figs (*con fichi*).

Soups: popular soups are mixed vegetable (*minestrone*), clear soup (*brodo*), and an interesting version with an egg beaten into it (*stracciatella*).

Pasta: traditionally served as an introductory course, not the main dish. Even the friendliest of restaurant owners will raise **107**

a sad eyebrow if you decide to make a whole meal out of a plate of spaghetti. It is said that there are as many different forms of Italian pasta as there are French cheeses – 360 at the last count, with new forms created every year. Each sauce, tomato, cheese, cream, meat or fish, needs its own noodle.

Besides spaghetti and macaroni, the worldwide popularity of pasta has familiarized us with *tagliatelle* ribbon noodles (known here as *fettuccine*), baked *lasagne* with layers of pasta, meat sauce and béchamel, rolled *cannelloni*, and *ravioli*. From there, you launch into the lusty poetry of *tortellini* and *cappelletti* (variations on *ravioli*), or curved *linguine*, flat *pappardelle*, quill-shaped *penne* and corrugated *rigatoni*. Discover the other 350 for yourselves.

Furthermore, there are almost as many sauces for pasta. The most famous, of course, is *bolognese*, or *ragù*. The tastiest version boasts not only minced beef, tomato purée and onions but chopped chicken livers, ham, carrots, celery, white wine and nutmeg. Other popular sauces are the simple *pomodoro* (tomato, garlic and basil), *aglio e olio* (garlic, olive oil and chilli peppers), *carbonara* (chopped bacon and eggs), *matriciana* (salt pork and tomato), *pesto* (basil and garlic ground in olive oil with pine nuts and parmesan cheese) and *vongole* (clams).

Pizza: another Italian invention familiar around the world, pizza is in reality a much more elaborate affair than you may be used to. Toppings generally include the following ingredients: tomato, ham, anchovies, cheese, mushrooms, peppers, artichoke hearts, egg, clams, tuna fish, garlic – or any other ingredient that takes the cook's fancy. It is especially popular after the opera or theatre.

Meat: most main courses will be a hearty meat dish. *Vitello* (veal) has pride of place, with the great speciality of Rome, *sal-timbocca* (literally 'jump in the mouth'), a veal roll with ham, sage and Marsala wine. Try the *costoletta* (pan-fried cutlet in breadcrumbs), or the *scaloppine al limone* (with lemon). *Osso buco* is a delicious dish of stewed veal shinbone in butter, with tomatoes, onions and mushrooms.

Manzo (beef), *maiale* (pork) and *agnello* (lamb) are most often served in straightforward style, charcoal-grilled or *al forno* (roasted). *Bistecca alla fiorentina* (grilled Florentine T-bone) is the emperor of all steaks and costs a royal ransom, but you should splash out and try it once. After that, the lesser proportions of the *bistecca* or *filetto* are something of an anticlimax.

Romans also claim the best *capretto* (roast kid), *porchetta* (suckling pig) – roasted whole on a spit – and *abbacchio* (spring lamb), flavoured with garlic, sage and rosemary, and seasoned just before serving with anchovy paste. The most common chicken dishes are *pollo alla diavola* (grilled) or *petti di pollo alla bolognese* (filleted with ham and cheese).

Fish: prepared in a simple way – grilled, steamed or fried. You should look out for *spigola* (seabass), *triglia* (red mullet), *pesce spada* (swordfish) and *coda di rospo* (angler fish). The *fritto misto* is mixed fried seafood, mostly shrimp and octopus.

Vegetables: these are ordered separately, as they do not automatically come with the meat dish. What is available will depend on the season, but you are most likely to find *spinaci* (spinach), *cicoria* (endives), *fagioli* (green beans in butter and garlic), *piselli* (peas) and *zucchini* (courgettes).

Aristocrats among cooked vegetables are the *funghi porcini* (big boletus mushrooms), which sometimes come stuffed (*ripieni*) with bacon, garlic, parsley and cheese. The white truffle is an autumn delicacy. Try also *peperonata* (red peppers stewed with tomatoes) or *melanzane* (aubergine) stuffed with anchovies, olives and capers. The Jewish Ghetto originated the spectacular *carciofi alla giudea* (whole artichokes, crisply fried – stem, heart, leaves and all).

109

A pizza chef has a colourful display at hand, not least a feast of grilled aubergines.

Cheeses: the famous *parmigiano* (Parmesan), far better than the exported product, is eaten separately, not just grated over soup or pasta. Try too blue *gorgonzola*, creamy *fontina*, pungent cow's milk *taleggio* or ewe's milk *pecorino*. *Ricotta* can be sweetened with sugar and cinnamon.

Dessert: usually means *gelati*, the creamiest ice-cream in the world. It's usually better in an ice-cream parlour (*gelateria*) than in the average *trattoria*. *Zuppa inglese* (literally 'English soup'), the Italian version of trifle, can be anything from an extremely thick and sumptuous mixture of fruit, cream, cake and Marsala to a disappointing sickly slice of cake.

You may prefer the coffee-flavoured trifle or *tirami sù* (literally 'pick me up'). *Zabaglione* (whipped egg yolks, sugar and Marsala) should be served warm or sent back. Fruit can be a succulent alternative: *fragole* (strawberries), served with whipped cream or lemon; *uva* (grapes), and *albicocche* (apricots).

DRINKS

Wine: all restaurants will offer the open wine of the house, red or white, in ¼, ½-litre or 1 litre carafes, as well as a good selection of bottled vintages.

Rome's 'local' wine comes from the surrounding province of Lazio. The whites from the Alban Hills, called Castelli Romani, are light and pleasant and can be sweet or dry. The most famous is Frascati. From further afield, the Chiantis of Tuscany are available everywhere; as are the velvety Valpolicella from the Veneto and Piedmont's full-bodied Barolo. Look out for the unusual Est! Est! Est! from Montefiascone on Lake Bolsena.

Italian beer: increasing in popularity but not as strong as north European brands. Italians will also order mineral water (*acqua minerale*) with their meal. Ask for it fizzy (*gassata*) or still (*naturale*).

Apéritif: bitters such as Campari and Punt e Mes are refreshing with soda and lemon. For after-dinner drinks, try the anis-flavoured *sambuca* with a *mosca* coffee-bean (literally a fly) swimming in it, or *grappa* distilled from grapes.

PRICES

While some restaurants offer fixed-price, three-course meals (*menu turistico* or *prezzo fisso*) which will save money, you'll almost always get better food by ordering individual dishes.

You should be warned that by law all restaurants must now issue a receipt indicating the value added tax (IVA). You may be stopped and fined if unable to show that the tax has been paid. The bill usually includes cover (*coperto*) and service (*servizio*).

To Help You Order...

Do you have a set menu? **Avete un menù a prezzo fisso?**
I'd like a/an/some... **Vorrei...**

beer	**una birra**	pepper	**del pepe**
bread	**del pane**	potatoes	**delle patate**
butter	**del burro**	salad	**un'insalata**
coffee	**un caffè**	salt	**del sale**
cream	**della panna**	soup	**una minestra**
fish	**del pesce**	sugar	**dello zucchero**
fruit	**della frutta**	tea	**un tè**
ice-cream	**un gelato**	(mineral)	**dell'acqua**
meat	**della carne**	water	**(minerale)**
milk	**del latte**	wine	**del vino**

...and Read the Menu

aglio	garlic	**lamponi**	raspberries
agnello	lamb	**maiale**	pork
albicocche	apricots	**manzo**	beef
aragosta	spiny lobster	**mela**	apple
arancia	orange	**melanzane**	aubergine
bistecca	beef steak	**merluzzo**	cod
braciola	chop	**ostriche**	oysters
bue	beef	**pesca**	peach
calamari	squid	**piselli**	peas
carciofi	artichokes	**pollo**	chicken
cavolo	cabbage	**pomodori**	tomatoes
cicoria	endive	**prosciutto**	ham
cipolle	onions	**rognoni**	kidneys
crostacei	shellfish	**tacchino**	turkey
fegato	liver	**uovo**	egg
formaggio	cheese	**uva**	grapes
frutti di mare	seafood	**vitello**	veal
112 funghi	mushrooms	**vongole**	clams

BLUEPRINT
for a
Perfect Trip

An A–Z Summary of Practical Information

Listed after some entries is the appropriate Italian translation, usually in the singular, plus a number of phrases that may come in handy during your stay in Italy.

ACCOMMODATION (See also CAMPING on p.116, YOUTH HOSTELS on p.141 and the list of RECOMMENDED HOTELS starting on p.66)

Rome's array of lodgings ranges from the simple and spartan to the decidedly palatial. Hotels are classified in five categories, graded from 1 to 5 stars, based on the amenities and comfort they offer. (The Rome Tourist Board no longer uses the term *pensione* in its classifications; these family-style boarding houses are now graded as hotels.) On its periphery, Rome has several motels. Some Roman Catholic institutions also take guests at reasonable rates.

In summer and at Easter, booking ahead is important, but for the rest of the year you can normally find accommodation in your preferred category without difficulty. The Rome Tourist Board (EPT) has up-to-date information at its offices in Via Parigi 5, at Fiumicino Airport and at Termini railway station. The EPT also has information offices at the (Roma-Nord) Salaria service area on the A1 *autostrada* (motorway) and at the (Roma-Sud) Frascati service area on the A2 *autostrada*.

If you plan to walk to most of Rome's sights, which is usually the best way, choose a hotel in the *centro storico* (historic centre – see p.23), rather than in the suburbs. The saving in transport costs and time should compensate for the slightly higher rates in the centre of town. Room rates quoted by all categories of hotels should be inclusive of taxes and service. Rates for 4- and 5-star hotels are also inclusive of air conditioning.

Rome has several 'daytime' hotels, one of them at Termini railway station. They provide bathrooms, hairdresser and left-luggage facilities.

I'd like a single/ double room.	**Vorrei una camera singola/ doppia**.
with bath/shower	**con bagno/doccia**
What's the rate per night?	**Qual è il prezzo per notte?**

AIRPORTS (*aeroporto*)

Rome is served by two airports, Leonardo da Vinci, commonly referred to as **Fiumicino**, 30km (18 miles) south west of the city, and **Ciampino**, 15km (9 miles) south east of the city on the Via Appia Nuova. Fiumicino handles mainly scheduled air traffic, while Ciampino is used by most charter companies. Fiumicino has two terminals, one for domestic use and the other for international flights, a 5- minute walk apart.

Fiumicino is connected by train with Roma Ostiense railway station; services operate at 20 to 30-minute intervals from 6.30am to 12.45am and the journey takes around 25 minutes. Roma Ostiense station connects with the Piramide stop on metro line B, which takes you into the city centre. Buses leave Ciampino every 30 minutes for Anagnina, where you can pick up the metro (line A) to Rome.

Airport information: Fiumicino, tel. 65951; Ciampino, tel. 794941.

B

BICYCLE AND MOTORCYCLE HIRE

You can hire bicycles from several locations, including the entrance to the metro at Piazza di Spagna and the Villa Borghese underground **115** park (lower level, third sector). A telephone hire service offers delivery at your hotel. Scooters and bicycles can be hired from Scoot-a-long, Via Cavour 302; tel. 6780206 and St. Peter Moto, Via di Porta Castello 43; tel. 6875714/6874909. You have to be over 21 years old to hire a scooter.

C ▬▬▬▬▬▬▬▬▬▬▬▬▬▬▬▬▬▬▬▬▬▬▬▬

CAMPING

Rome and the surrounding countryside have some 20 official camp-sites, mostly equipped with electricity, water and toilet facilities. They are listed in the telephone directory under 'Campeggio-Ostelli-Villaggi Turistici', or contact Roma Camping, Via Aurelia 831; tel. 6623018. You can also contact the Tourist Office for a comprehensive list of sites and rates. The Touring Club Italiano (TCI) and the Automobile Club d'Italia (ACI) publish lists of campsites and tourist villages, available at bookstores or the Tourist Office. You are strongly advised to stick to the official sites.

If you enter Italy with a caravan, you should be able to show an inventory (with two copies) of the material and equipment in the caravan, eg. dishes and linen.

Is there a campsite near here?   **C'è un campeggio qui vicino?**

We have a tent/caravan (trailer).   **Abbiamo la tenda/la roulotte**.

CAR HIRE (*autonoleggio*)

The major car hire firms have offices at the airports as well as in the city; they are listed in the telephone directory. It is possible to rent a car in one Italian city and give it up in another. To rent a car you must be at least 21 years of age and have held a valid driver's licence for at least a year. Mandatory third-party insurance is included in the rates. Note that hiring a car is expensive in Italy. It may be cheaper and more convenient to arrange car hire in advance through your automobile association or a company in your home country, or as part of a fly-drive package.

'd like to rent a car (tomorrow).	**Vorrei noleggiare una macchina (per domani).**
'or one day	**per un giorno**
'or one week	**per una settimana**

CLIMATE

From mid-June to mid-September, temperatures in Rome range from hot to very hot. Winters are cool, even cold, and at times rainy, with occasional snow – but often you will find the sun does shine. Spring and autumn are pleasantly mild.

		J	F	M	A	M	J	J	A	S	O	N	D
Max	°F	52	55	59	66	74	82	87	86	79	71	61	55
	°C	11	13	15	19	23	28	30	30	26	22	16	13
Min	°F	40	42	45	50	56	63	67	67	62	55	49	44
	°C	5	5	7	10	13	17	20	20	17	13	9	6

*Minimum temperatures are measured just before sunrise, maximum temperatures in the afternoon.

COMPLAINTS (*reclamo*)

In hotels, shops and restaurants, complaints should be made to the manager (*direttore*) or the proprietor (*proprietario*). If satisfaction is not quickly forthcoming, make clear your intention to report the incident to the Tourist Office (see p.140), or to the police (see p.132) for more serious matters. Arguments over taxi fares can usually be settled by checking the notices in taxis specifying supplementary charges (airport runs, night surcharges, etc). It is generally advisable to try to reach an agreement over price in advance.

CONSULATES (*consolato*)

Contact the offices of your diplomatic representative if you lose your passport or run into serious trouble. The consulate can also provide lists of doctors, lawyers and interpreters. These are the main consulate offices for English-speaking visitors:

Australia: Viale Alessandria 215; tel. 832721.

Canada: Via Zara 30; tel. 4403028.

Eire: Laargo Nazareno 3; tel. 6782541.

New Zealand: Via Zara 28; tel. 4402928.

South Africa: Via Tanaro 14/16; tel. 8419794.

UK: Via XX Settembre 80/a; tel. 4825441.

USA: Via Vittorio Veneto 121; tel. 46741.

CRIME

Petty theft is an endless annoyance, but cases of violence against tourists are rare. It's wise to leave any documents you don't need and excess cash in the hotel safe and keep what you take with you, including credit cards, in an inside pocket or a pouch inside your clothes. Handbags are particularly vulnerable, so be attentive on crowded public transport or in secluded streets. Beware of begging gypsy children and don't let them distract your attention for a moment; they are very adept pickpockets. It's a good idea to make photocopies of your tickets, driving licence, passport and other vital documents to facilitate reporting any theft and obtaining replacements.

If you park your car, lock it and empty it of everything, with the glove compartment open, to discourage prospective thieves. Wherever possible, try to park in a garage or attended parking area.

If you are robbed, report the theft to the police, so that you have a statement to file with your insurance claim. The central police station is at: Questura Centrale, Via San Vitale 15; tel. 4686.

I want to report a theft. **Voglio denunciare un furto.**

| My wallet/handbag/passport/ ticket has been stolen. | **Mi hanno rubato il portafoglio/la borsa/il passaporto/il biglietto**. |

CUSTOMS AND ENTRY FORMALITIES

For a stay of up to three months, a valid passport is sufficient for citizens of Australia, Canada, New Zealand and the United States. Visitors from Eire, the United Kingdom and other EU countries need only an identity card to enter Italy. Tourists from South Africa must have a visa.

Here are some of the main items you can take into Italy duty-free and, when returning home, back to your own country:

Into:	Cigarettes		Cigars		Tobacco	Spirits		Wine
Italy [1]	200	or	50	or	250g	1 l	and	2 l
Australia	200	or	250 g	or	250 g	1 l	or	1 l
Canada	200	and	50	and	900 g	1.1 l	or	1.1 l
Eire	200	or	50	or	250 g	1 l	and	2 l
N Zealand	200	or	50	or	250 g	1.1 l	and	4.5 l
S Africa	400	and	50	and	250 g	1 l	and	2 l
UK	400	or	100	or	500 g	1 l	and	2 l
USA	200	and	100	and	[2]	1 l	or	1 l
Within the EC [3]	800	and	200	and	1kg	10 l	and	90 l

1) For non-European residents or residents outside the EU or from duty-free shops within EU countries.
2) a reasonable quantity
3) Guidelines for non duty-free within the EU. For the import of larger amounts you must be able to prove that the goods are for your own personal use. For EU duty free allowances see [1] above.

Currency restrictions. As a foreign tourist, you may import unlimited amounts in local or other currencies, but to take more than L20,000,000 or the equivalent in foreign money out again, you must fill in a V2 declaration form at the border when you arrive.

I've nothing to declare.	**Non ho nulla da dichiarare**.
It's for my personal use.	**Per mio uso personale**.

D

DISABLED VISITORS

Cobblestone streets and steep hills are just two of the problems facing travellers with disabilities visiting Rome. Facilities for the disabled in the city are still thin on the ground, but there are signs that the authorities are beginning to take steps to remedy this. There are lavatories for disabled people at both the main airports, and at Stazione Termini and Piazza San Pietro. St Peter's and the Vatican Museums are wheelchair-accessible, but unfortunately this is not yet the case with many of the city's other major museums and galleries. Up-to-date information on access to museums and monuments is provided by the Rome Tourist Board's free leaflet, *Musei e Monumenti di Roma*. The Milan-based Harvey Club (Via Luosi 38, 20131 Milan; tel. 02-2614 1600) arranges tours for disabled people in Italy and also provides information and advice.

DRIVING

Entering Italy. To bring your car into Italy, you will need:

- an international driving licence or valid national one
- car registration papers
- green card (an extension to your regular insurance policy, making it valid specifically for Italy)
- a red warning triangle in case of breakdown
- national identity sticker for your car

Drivers of cars that are not their own must have the owner's written permission. Before leaving home, check with your automobile association about the latest regulations concerning petrol coupons (these give tourists access to cheaper fuel) in Italy, as these are constantly changing.

Speed limits on the *autostrade* toll highways are 130kph (80mph); on other roads the limit is 90kph (55mph). The limit in built-up areas is generally 60kph (37.5mph).

Driving conditions. Seat belts are compulsory. Drive on the right, pass on the left. Traffic on major roads has right of way over that entering from side roads, but this is frequently ignored, so be very careful. At intersections of roads of similar importance the car on the right theoretically has the right of way. When passing other vehicles, or remaining in the left-hand (passing) lane, keep your directional indicator flashing.

Motorways are designed for fast and safe driving; a toll is collected for each section. Take a ticket from an automatic machine or from the booth attendant and pay at the other end according to the distance you have travelled.

Driving in Rome. Only the most intrepid motorist stays cool in the face of the Romans' hair-raising driving habits. However, Roman drivers are not reckless – simply attuned to a different concept of driving. If you observe the following ground rules and venture with prudence into the urban traffic whirlpool, you stand a good chance of coming out unscathed.

Glance round to right and left and in your rear-view mirror all the time; other drivers are doing the same, and they've developed quick reflexes. Treat traffic lights which are theoretically in your favour and white lines across merging side streets with caution – don't take priority for granted. To make progress in a traffic jam in one of Rome's squares, inch gently but confidently forward into the snarl-up. Waving on another driver, courteously letting him or her cut in ahead of you, is tantamount to abdicating your rights as a motorist. **121**

Most of the city centre between the river, Piazza del Popolo, Piazza di Spagna and Piazza Venezia is closed to traffic all day, except for taxis, buses and cars with special permits.

Traffic police (*polizia stradale*). The traffic police patrol the highways and byways on motorcycles or in Alfa Romeos, usually light blue. Speeding fines often have to be paid on the spot – ask for a receipt (*ricevuta*). All cities and many towns and villages have signs posted at the outskirts indicating the telephone number of the local traffic police or *carabinieri*. The headquarters in Rome are at Viale Romania 45, tel. 80981.

Breakdowns. Call boxes are located at regular intervals on the *autostrade* in case of breakdowns or other emergencies. You can dial 116 for breakdown service from the ACI. Temporary membership of the ACI can be taken out at main frontier posts.

Fuel and oil. Service stations abound in Italy, usually with at least one mechanic on duty. Most stations close on Sundays, and also every day from noon to 3pm. Stations along the *autostrade* are open 24 hours a day. Fuel (*benzina*) is sold at government-set prices and comes in super (98-100 octane), lead-free (95-octane), normal (86-88-octane) and diesel. Unleaded petrol is now also common. Look for the pumps with green labels marked *senza piombo* (without lead) or the abbreviation SP.

Fluid measures

Distance

122

Parking (See also CRIME on p.118). For motorized tourists as well as residents, parking is one of Rome's greatest challenges. Your wisest course is to find a legal parking place near your hotel for the duration of your stay and see the city on foot or by public transport. If you park in a tow-away zone, you may have to pay a heavy fine and spend many hours getting your car released from the tow park. If your car is towed away, contact the *vigili urbani* (municipal police) central headquarters at Via Consolazione 4 (tel. 67691), for instructions.

Road signs. Most road signs employed in Italy are the international pictographs, but here are some written ones you may come across:

Accendere le luci	Use headlights
Deviazione	Diversion (Detour)
Divieto di sorpasso	No overtaking (passing)
Divieto di sosta	No stopping
Lavori in corso	Roadworks
Passaggio a livello	Level crossing
Pericolo	Danger
Rallentare	Slow down
Senso unico	One-way street
Senso vietato/Vietato l'inresso	No entry
Zona pedonale	Pedestrian zone
driving licence	**patente**
car registration papers	**libretto di circolazione**
green card	**carta verde**
Where's the nearest car park?	**Dov'è il parcheggio più vicino?**
Can I park here?	**Posso parcheggiare qui?**

Are we on the right road for...?	**Siamo sulla strada giusta per...?**
Fill the tank, please.	**Per favore, faccia il pieno.**
super/normal	**super/normale**
unleaded	**senza piombo**
diesel	**gasolio**
Check the oil/tyres/battery.	**Controlli l'olio/i pneumatici/la batteria.**
I've had a breakdown.	**Ho avuto un guasto.**
There's been an accident.	**C'è stato un incidente.**

ELECTRIC CURRENT

Electric current is 220 volts, 50 Hz AC. Bring a multiple adaptor plug (*una presa multipla*), or buy one as required.

EMERGENCIES

In an emergency you can phone the following numbers all over Italy 24 hours a day:

Emergency services (ambulance, fire, police): **113**

Carabinieri (for urgent police action): **112**

Fire: **115**

Road assistance (ACI): **116**

Here are some further useful phrases that you hopefully won't need to employ:

Careful!	**Attenzione!**
Fire!	**Incendio!**
Help!	**Aiuto!**
Stop thief!	**Al ladro!**

On entering and leaving a shop, restaurant or office, the expected greeting is *buon giorno* (good morning) or *buona sera* (good evening). When approaching anyone with an enquiry, the correct form is *per favore* (please), and for any service say *grazie* (thanks), to which the reply is *prego* (don't mention it/you're welcome).

Introductions are usually accompanied by handshaking and the phrase *piacere* (it's a pleasure). With people you know well, *ciao* is the casual form of greeting or farewell. *Salve* is a casual form of farewell less intimate than *ciao*. When wished *buon appetito* before a meal, reply *grazie, altrettanto* (thank you, and the same to you).

How are you?	**Come sta?**
Very well, thanks.	**Molto bene, grazie.**

GETTING TO ROME

If the choice of ways to go is bewildering, the complexity of fares and regulations can be downright stupefying. A reliable travel agent will have full details of all the latest flight possibilities, fares and regulations.

By Air: Rome's Fiumicino (Leonardo da Vinci) Airport is on intercontinental air routes and is linked by frequent services to cities in Europe, North America, the Middle East and Africa. Average flying times are: New York–Rome 8 hours; Los Angeles–Rome 15 hours; London–Rome 2½ hours; Sydney–Rome 26 hours.

By Car: Cross-Channel car ferries link the UK with France, Belgium and Holland. Once on the continent, you can put your car on a train to Milan (starting points include Boulogne, Paris, and Cologne). Alternatively you can drive from the Channel coast to Rome without leaving a motorway. The main north-south (Milan–Florence–Reggio di Calabria) and east-west (L'Aquila–Civitavecchia) motorways connect with Rome via a huge ring motorway (*grande raccordo anulare*).

125

By Rail: **Inter-Rail** cards are valid in Italy, as is the **Eurailpass** for non-European residents (sign up before you leave home). Within Italy, you can obtain an **Italian Tourist Ticket** (*Biglietto Turistico di Libera Circolazione*) for unlimited first or second-class rail travel for 8, 15, 21 or 30 days.

The **Freedom Pass** from Euro-Domino offers travel on any 3, 5 or 10 days within one month in several European countries. For further enquiries write or call at the International Rail Centre, Victoria Station, London SW1Y 1JY or telephone 071-834 23445.

The **Kilometric Ticket** (*Biglietto Chilometrico*) can be used by up to five people and is valid for 20 trips or 3,000km (1,860 miles), first or second class, over a period of two months.

GUIDES AND TOURS

Most hotels in Rome can arrange for multilingual guides or interpreters. At some museums and sites, taped tour commentaries can be rented. The Italian Tourist Agency, CIT, Piazza della Repubblica 68 (tel. 47941), and many private firms offer tours of all the major sites, plus excursions to other points of interest. Often tourists are picked up and dropped off at their hotels.

ATAC, Rome's municipal bus company, provides an inexpensive 3-hour sightseeing tour which takes in many of the major sites. Tours on ATAC bus 110 depart from Piazza dei Cinquecento; tickets are available from the ATAC information booth in the square.

LANGUAGE

Italians appreciate foreigners making an effort to speak their language, even if it's only a few words. In the major hotels and shops, staff usually speak some English.

Bear in mind the following tips on pronunciation:

- 'c' is pronounced like ch in change when it is followed by an 'e' or an 'i'.
- 'ch' together sounds like the 'c' in cat.
- 'g' followed by an 'e' or an 'i' is pronounced like 'j' in jet.
- 'gh' together sounds like the 'g' in gap.
- 'gl' together sounds like the 'lli' in million.
- 'gn' is pronounced like 'ni' in onion.
- 'sc'+ i pronounced like 'she'.

The Berlitz phrase book *Italian for Travellers* covers all the situations you are likely to encounter in Italy; also useful is the Italian-English/English-Italian pocket dictionary, complete with a menu-reader supplement. For further useful expressions, see the front cover of this guide.

LAUNDRY AND DRY-CLEANING

Most hotels handle laundry and dry-cleaning. Naturally it is cheaper to do your own washing (or leave it with the attendant) at a *lavanderia* or hand it in at a *tintoria*, which usually offers a normal or express service.

When will it be ready?	**Quando sarà pronto?**
I must have this for tomorrow morning.	**Mi serve per domani mattina.**

LOST PROPERTY

Cynics believe that anything lost in Italy is lost forever, but that's not necessarily true in Rome. Restaurants will more often than not have the 'lost' briefcase, guidebook or camera waiting for you at the cashier's desk. If you're not sure where the loss occurred, have your hotel receptionist call the lost property office (*ufficio oggetti rinvenuti* or *smarriti*). Report lost documents to the police (see p.132) or your consulate (see p.118).

Rome's general lost property office is the Ufficio Oggetti Rinvenuti at Via Bettoni 1; tel. 5816040. There are lost property offices **127** at the Termini railway station (tel. 47301) and at ATAC in Via Bettoni 1; tel. 5816040. For losses on the metro call 5753 3620.

I've lost my passport/ wallet/handbag.	**Ho perso il passaporto/ portafoglio/la borsetta.**

MAPS (*pianta*)

The offices of the Rome Tourist Board give away basic street plans featuring a selection of local information. More detailed maps are on sale at news-stands. A useful bus network map is sold at the ATAC information booth in Piazza dei Cinquecento.

MEDICAL CARE

If your health insurance policy does not cover you while abroad, take out a short-term policy before leaving home. Visitors from EU countries carrying the E111 form available from their local post office are entitled to emergency medical and hospital treatment under the Italian social security system. The E111 form explains the steps you will need to take to obtain treatment in Italy.

If you need medical care, ask your hotel receptionist to help you find a doctor (or dentist) who speaks English. Both the US and British consulates (see p.118) have lists of English-speaking doctors. Local Health Units of the Italian National Health Service are listed in the phone directory under *Unità Sanitaria Locale*. The first-aid (*pronto soccorso*) section of hospitals handles medical emergencies.

Pharmacies. The Italian *farmacia* is open during shopping hours (see OPENING HOURS on p.130). Usually one operates at night and on weekends for each district on a rota basis. The opening schedule for duty pharmacies is posted on every pharmacy door and in the local newspapers. We advise you to bring along with you an adequate supply of any prescribed medication, particularly since new laws have made prescriptions mandatory for many medicines.

I need a doctor/a dentist.	**Ho bisogno di un medico/ dentista.**
Where's the nearest (all-night) chemist?	**Dov'è la farmacia (di turno) più vicina?**

MONEY MATTERS (See also OPENING HOURS on p.130)

Currency. Italy's monetary unit is the *lira* (plural *lire*, abbreviated L or Lit).

Coins: L10, 20, 50, 100, 200, 500.

Notes: L1,000, 2,000, 5,000, 10,000, 50,000, 100,000.

For currency restrictions, see CUSTOMS AND ENTRY FORMALITIES on p.120.

Currency exchange. Currency exchange offices (*cambio*) are usually open from 9am to 1.30pm and 2.30 to 6pm. Many are closed on Saturday. Exchange rates here are less advantageous than those offered by banks. A flat rate of commission is common, so it is not worth changing small amounts frequently. Passports are sometimes required when changing money.

Credit cards and traveller's cheques. Most hotels, many shops, and some restaurants take credit cards. Traveller's cheques are accepted almost everywhere, but you will get better value if you exchange your cheques for lire at a bank or *cambio*. Passports are required when cashing cheques. Eurocheques are fairly easily cashed in Italy.

I want to change some pounds/dollars.	**Desidero cambiare delle sterline/dei dollari.**
Do you accept traveller's cheques?	**Accetta traveller's cheques?**
Can I pay with this credit card?	**Posso pagare con la carta di credito?**

NEWSPAPERS AND MAGAZINES

A good selection of British and international English-language newspapers and magazines are on sale, sometimes a day late, at the airport and main railway station, and at news-stands in the city centre. Prices are high for all foreign publications.

The supplement *Trovaroma*, published in the Thursday edition of the newspaper *La Repubblica*, provides comprehensive listings of cultural events in Rome. The monthly *Carnet di Roma*, published by the Rome Tourist Board in Italian, English, French and German, also lists events, as does the fortnightly English-language publication *Wanted in Rome*, available in Rome's English bookshops.

Have you any English-language newspapers? **Aveti giornali in inglese?**

OPENING HOURS

Even within Rome, opening hours vary. In true Mediterranean fashion, much of the city shuts or slows down after lunch. However, for some offices the modern non-stop business day is gradually creeping in. The following is therefore just a guideline.

Shops. Open 9am to 1pm and 4 to 8pm (summer hours) and until 7.30pm (winter hours), Monday to Saturday (half-day closing is usually Monday morning); food stores open 7am to 1.30pm and 4 to 7.30pm in the winter and 8pm in the summer (half-day closing usually Thursday afternoon). Tourist resort shops stay open all day, every day, in high season.

Post offices. Normally open 8.30am to 5.30pm, Monday to Friday, until noon on Saturday. The main post office in Piazza San Silvestro **130** stays open until 9pm. Closed on Sundays.

Banks. 8.30am to 1.30pm and again for an hour or so in the afternoon, Monday to Friday.

Principal businesses. 8 or 9am to 1 or 1.30pm and 4, 4.30 or 5 to 7, 7.30 or 8pm, Monday to Saturday. Sometimes they are closed Saturday afternoon.

Pharmacies. 8.30am to 1pm and 4 to 8pm.

Churches are generally open from early morning to 12 or 12.30pm, and from 4 or 5 to 7pm. St Peter's and some of the larger basilicas remain open all day.

Museums and historic sites. These are usually open Tuesday to Sunday, from 9am to 2pm (if not earlier), and, in some cases, also from 5 to 8pm. Closing day is usually Monday; if Monday is a public holiday (see p.133), some museums close the following day.

The following museums and sights are open on Monday: Vatican museum, closed Sunday; Castel Sant'Angelo open every morning, and Monday and Thursday till 6pm; Keats–Shelley Memorial house, open every weekday; Catacombs of St Calixtus, closed Wednesday; Catacombs of St Sebastian, closed Thursday; Colosseum, closed Wednesday and Saturday.

P

PLANNING YOUR BUDGET

To give you an idea of what to expect, here's a list of average prices in *lire* (L). However, remember that all prices must be regarded as approximate.

Airport transfer. Train from Fiumicino Airport to Roma Ostiense railway station L6,000, then metro to Termini central railway station L800. Bus from Ciampino Airport to Anagnina Metro station L1,000. Taxi from Fiumicino to city centre L50,000-60,000.

Baby-sitters. L12,000 per hour, transport and agency fee are usually included in the price.

Buses (city) **and metro**. Standard fare L1200 for buses (valid for 90 minutes) and L1000 for the Metro; Day ticket for buses and Metro (biglietto integrato) L4000

Camping. L8,000 per person per night, caravan (trailer) or camper L8,000, tent L5,000, car L4,000, motorbike L2,000.

Car hire. *Fiat Panda 45* L120,000 per day with unlimited mileage, L550,000 per week with unlimited mileage. *Alfa 33* L170,000 per day with unlimited mileage, L750,000 per week with unlimited mileage.

Cigarettes (packet of 20). Italian brands L2,450 and up, imported brands L3,500.

Entertainment. Cinema L10,000, discotheque (entry and first drink) L20,000-30,000, outdoor opera L30,000-90,000.

Hairdressers. Woman's shampoo and set or blow dry L30,000-50,000, permanent wave L100,000-120,000. Man's haircut L15,000-25,000, with shampoo L20,000-40,000.

Hotels (double room with bath, including tax and service). 5-star L500,000-650,000, 4-star L260,000-500,000, 3-star L140,000-260,000, 2-star L90,000-140,000, 1-star L50,000-90,000.

Meals and drinks. Continental breakfast L5,000, lunch/dinner in fairly good establishment L35,000-50,000, coffee served at a table L3,000-5,000, served at the bar L900-1,500, bottle of beer L3,000-6,000, soft drinks L1,500-3,000, aperitif L5,000 and up.

Museums. L2,000-10,000.

Shopping bag. 500g of bread L1,000 and up, 250g of butter L2,500 and up, 6 eggs L1,200 and up, 500g of beefsteak L11,000, 200g of coffee L3,000 and up, bottle of wine L3,500 and up.

Taxis. Minimum charge L6,400 for the first 9 minutes or 3km (1.8 miles), L300 for each successive 45 seconds. Surcharge for night-time, holidays, and each piece of luggage L1,000-3,000.

POLICE

The municipal police (*vigili urbani*), dressed in navy blue or summer white uniforms with white helmets, handle city traffic and other city police tasks. They are courteous and helpful to tourists, though they rarely speak a foreign language. Those who do act as interpreters display a special badge on their uniforms, which indicates the languages they speak.

The *carabinieri*, dressed in dark blue uniforms with a red stripe down the side of the trousers, deal with theft, more serious crimes, demonstrations and military affairs. The national, or state, police (*polizia di stato*) are distinguished by their navy blue jackets and light blue trousers, and handle other police and administrative matters. (For traffic police details see also DRIVING on p.120). The all-purpose emergency number, **113**, will get you police assistance.

Where's the nearest **Dov'è il più vicino**
police station? **posto di polizia?**

POST OFFICES (*posta* or *ufficio postale*)

Post offices handle telegrams, mail and money transfers. Look for the yellow sign with PT in black. Postage stamps are also sold at tobacconists and at some hotel desks. Post boxes are red; the slot marked *Per la Città* is for local mail only; the one labelled *Altre Destinazioni* is for all other destinations. Post to and from Rome can be slow. The Vatican post is more efficient; buy Vatican stamps near the Tourist Office in St Peter's Square and use the post boxes there.

For a short stay it is not worth arranging to receive mail. However, there is a *poste restante* service at the main post office in Piazza San Silvestro. Don't forget your passport for identification when you go to pick up mail. You will have to pay a small fee.

Telegrams (*telegramme*) can be sent to destinations inside and outside Italy, as can telex messages. There is now a rapidly growing facsimile service.

PUBLIC HOLIDAYS (*festa*)

Banks, government offices, and most shops and museums close on public holidays. When one falls on a Thursday or a Tuesday, Italians may make a *ponte* (bridge) to the weekend, meaning that Friday or Monday is taken off as well.

1 January	*Capodanno*	New Year's Day
6 January	*Epifania*	Epiphany
25 April	*Festa della Liberazione*	Liberation Day
1 May	*Primo Maggio*	May Day
15 August	*Ferragosto*	Assumption Day
1 November	*Ognissanti*	All Saints' Day
8 December	*L'Immacolata Concezione*	Immaculate Conception
25 December	*Natale*	Christmas Day
26 December	*Santo Stefano*	St Stephen's Day
Moveable date:	*Lunedì di Pasqua*	Easter Monday

In addition, Rome has a local holiday on 29 June, the *Festa di San Pietro e San Paolo*, the Feast of Saints Peter and Paul, the city's patron saints, when everything closes. Get to St Peter's Square early if you want to be a part of this as there are huge crowds.

PUBLIC TRANSPORT (See also TAXIS on p.137)

Underground/Subway (*metropolitana* or *metrò*). Rome has two underground railway lines. Line A runs from Via Ottaviano near the Vatican south east to Via Anagnina, stopping at more than 20 stations and passing close to many of Rome's popular tourist sights. The intersecting Line B runs from Rebibbia in the north east of the city through Stazione Termini to EUR in the south west. Some trains branch off at Magliana and go on to the coast, reaching Ostia Antica and Lido di Ostia. Metro stations are identified by a large red sign containing a white letter M. Tickets are sold at news-stands and tobacconists, or can be purchased from machines at the stations.

Buses (*autobus*). Rome's fleet of orange buses serves every corner of the city. Although crowded on certain routes and at rush hours, they are an inexpensive way of crossing the city. Each bus stop (*fermata*) indicates the numbers of the buses stopping there and the routes they serve. Tickets for buses must be bought in advance from news-stands or tobacconists. Enter by the rear doors and punch your ticket in a machine; exit by the middle doors. A single ticket is valid for 90 minutes and can be used on as many buses as you like within that period. A *biglietto integrato* (BIG) lets you travel all day on buses and the metro; a cheaper ticket is valid for half the day. Weekly tickets are sold at the ATAC (transport authority) information booth in Piazza dei Cinquecento, in front of Stazione Termini. Network maps are available from the ATAC booth and from news-stands. ACOTRAL (tel. 591 5551) operates bus services to the outskirts of Rome.

Horse-cabs (*carrozzelle*). A familiar sight in Rome for centuries, horse-drawn carriages now number only a few dozen. They can be found at many of the major tourist sites across the city, including St Peter's Square, the Spanish Steps and the Colosseum. A complete tour around the centre of the city will cost you around L150,000.

Trains. The Italian State Railways (*Ferrovie dello Stato* – FS) operate an extensive network all over the country. Although fares have been rising in recent years, they are still among the lowest in Europe. Choose your train carefully, as journey times (and ticket prices) vary a good deal. The following list describes the various types of train:
Eurocity (*EC*); international express, first class only, reservation and surcharge.
Intercity (*IC*)/*Rapido*; high-speed super-express, first and second class, reservation and surcharge.
Espresso (*Epr*); long-distance trains stopping at main stations.
Diretto (*Dir*); slower than the Espresso, makes local stops.
Locale (*L*); local train which stops at almost every station.
Metropolitana (*servizi dedicati*); connecting service from airports and cities to major cities.

Children under the age of 12 travel half price; those under the age of 4 years (not occupying a seat) travel free.

Tickets can be purchased and reservations made at a local travel agency or at the railway station. Better class trains have dining-cars or self-service cars which offer refreshments at reasonable prices. If you don't have a reservation, you should arrive at the station at least 20 minutes before departure; Italy's trains are often crowded.

Where's the nearest bus stop/ underground station?	**Dov'è la fermata d'autobus/ la stazione della metropolitana più vicina?**
When's the next bus/train to...?	**Quando parte il prossimo autobus/treno per...?**
I'd like a ticket to...	**Vorrei un biglietto per...**
single (one-way)	**andata**
return (round-trip)	**andata e ritorno**

R

RADIO AND TV (*radio, televisione*)

The RAI, Italy's state broadcasting system, has three TV channels. There are also numerous private national and local channels. CBS news from the previous evening is broadcast each morning at 7am from Tuesday to Saturday on Telemontecarlo. During the tourist season, RAI radio broadcasts news in English at 10am Monday-Saturday and at 9.30am on Sunday. Vatican Radio carries foreign-language religious news programmes. British (BBC), American (VOA) and Canadian (CBC) programmes are easily obtained on short-wave transistor radios.

RELIGION

Roman Catholic mass is celebrated daily and several times on Sunday in Italian. A few churches have occasional services in English. Confessions are heard in English in St Peter's, Santa Maria Maggiore, St John Lateran, St Paul's Outside the Walls and a number of other churches.

A number of non-Catholic denominations have congregations in Rome with services in English, including Anglican at All Saints, Via del Babuino 153; American Episcopal at St Paul's, Via Nazionale; Scottish Presbyterian at St Andrew's, Via XX Settembre 7; Methodist at Via Firenze 38. The Jewish Synagogue is at Lungotevere Cenci 9. The city's first mosque is in Via del Forte Antenne.

T

TAXIS (*tassì* or *taxi*)

Rome's licensed yellow and white taxis may be picked up at a taxi rank (on all the major piazzas) or summoned by telephone. When you phone for a taxi, you pay a surcharge. Extra fees are also charged for luggage, night, holiday or airport trips: the rates are posted in four languages inside all taxis. A tip of at least 10 percent is customary. Beware of the non-metred unlicensed taxis (*abusivi*), which charge much more than the normal taxi rates for trips in private cars.

TELEPHONES (*telefono*)

Public telephone booths are scattered at strategic locations throughout the city. Calls can also be made from bars and cafés, indicated by a yellow telephone sign showing a telephone dial and receiver. The main public telephone office, in the Palazzo delle Poste in Piazza San Silvestro, is open from 8am to midnight.

Older types of public payphones require tokens (*gettoni*) with a value of L200 (available at bars, hotels, post offices and tobacconists); modern ones, with three slots, take both tokens and 100, 200 and 500-lire coins.

From telephones labelled *Teleselezione* you can make direct international calls, but be sure to have a good supply of coins or tokens. Some telephones will take phone cards (*scheda telefonica*) to the value of 5,000 or 10,000 lire, available from bars and shops and at SIP (Italian Telephone Service) offices. If you make a long-distance call from a hotel expect to be heavily surcharged.

To make a call from a pay phone, insert the token or coin and lift the receiver. The normal dialling tone is a series of long dash sounds. **137**

A dot-dot-dot series means the central computer is overloaded; hang up and try again.

The English-speaking operators of the ACI's telephone assistance service provide tourists with information and advice. Dial **116**.

Some useful numbers:

Local directory and other Italian enquiries: **12**

European international operator: **15**

Intercontinental operator: **170**

Direct dialling for Australia: 0061, Canada: 001, Eire: 0035, South Africa: 0027, UK: 0044, USA: 001.

Give me ... tokens, please.	**Per favore, mi dia ... gettoni.**
Can you get me this number in...?	**Può passarmi questo numero a...?**
I'd like a stamp for this letter/ postcard.	**Desidero un francobollo per questa lettera/cartolina.**

TIME DIFFERENCES

Italy follows Central European Time (GMT + 1). From the last Sunday in March to the last Sunday in September, clocks are put ahead one hour (GMT + 2).

Summer Time Chart:

New York	London	**Italy**	Jo'burg	Sydney	Auckland
6am	11am	**noon**	noon	8pm	10pm

TIPPING

Though a service charge is added to most restaurant bills it is customary to leave an additional tip. It is also in order to hand porters, doormen, garage attendants etc. a little something for their services. The chart over the page will give you some guidelines:

Hotel porter, per bag	L2,000 to L5,000
Hotel maid, per day	L2,000 to L5,000
Lavatory attendant	L1000 or L2000
138 Waiter	5-10 percent

Taxi driver	10 percent
Hairdresser/barber	up to 15 percent
Tour guide	10 percent

TOILETS

Most museums and art galleries have public toilets. Bars, restaurants, cafés, large stores, airports, railway stations and car-parks all have facilities. On the whole they are clean and in good order, but you should carry your own tissues.

Toilets may be labelled with a symbol of a man or a woman or the initials W.C. Sometimes the wording will be in Italian, but beware, as you might be misled: *Uomini* is for men, *Donne* for women. Equally, *Signori* with a final 'i' is for men, but *Signore* with a final 'e' means women.

TOURIST INFORMATION OFFICES

The Italian National Tourist Office (*Ente Nazionale Italiano per il Turismo*, abbreviated ENIT) is represented in Italy and abroad. They publish detailed brochures with up-to-date information on accommodation, means of transport, general tips and useful addresses for the whole country.

Australia and New Zealand: c/o Italian Government Tourist Office, Lions Building, 1-1-2 Moto Akasaka, Minato Ku, Tokyo 107; tel. (03) 3478 2051.

Canada: Italian Government Travel Office, Suite 2414, 1 Place Ville-Marie, Montreal, Quebec, H3B 3M9; tel. (514) 866 7667.

Eire: Italian State Tourist Office, 47 Merrion Square, Dublin 2; tel. (01) 766 397.

South Africa: Italian State Tourist Office, PO Box 6507, Johannesburg 2000.

United Kingdom: Italian State Tourist Office, 1 Princes Street, London W1R 8AY; tel. (071) 408 1254.

Government Travel Office, Suite 1565, 630 Fifth Av-
York, NY 10111, tel. (212) 245 4822; Italian Government
fice, Suite 1046, 500 North Michigan Avenue, Chicago, IL
tel. (312) 644 0990; Italian Government Travel Office, Suite
12400 Wilshire Boulevard, Los Angeles CA 90025, tel. (310)
0098.

The Tourist Office headquarters in **Rome** are at Via Parigi 11; tel.
488 1851 and Via Parigi 5 (Tourist Assistance); tel. 488 3748, with
branches at Stazione Termini and Fiumicino Airport.

| Where's the tourist office? | **Dov'è l'ufficio turistico?** |

WATER
Rome's drinking water, not least from its outdoor fountains, is famous for its flavour and perfectly safe. Nonetheless, with meals it is
customary to drink bottled mineral water. If tap water is not drink-
able it will usually carry a sign saying *acqua non potabile*.

| I'd like a bottle of mineral water. | **Vorrei una bottiglia di acqua minerale.** |
| carbonated/still | **gassata/naturale** |

WEIGHTS AND MEASURES
(For fluid and distance measures, see DRIVING on p.122.)

Weight

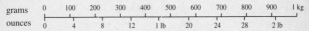

Temperature

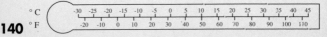

Length

cm	0	5	10	15	20	25	30
inches	0		2	4	6	8	10	12

metres	0		1 m		2 m
ft/yd	0	1 ft	1 yd		2 yd

YOUTH HOSTELS (*ostello della gioventù*)

Youth hostels are open to holders of membership cards issued by the International Youth Hostels Federation, or by the AIG (*Associazione Italiana Alberghi per la Gioventù*), the Italian Youth Hostels Association, at: Via Cavour 44, 00184 Rome; tel. (06) 4871152; fax 4880492. Open Monday to Thursday 8am-5pm, Friday 8am-3pm.

SOME USEFUL EXPRESSIONS

(see also the cover of this guide for further useful expressions)

where/when/how	**dove/quando/como**
yesterday/today/tomorrow	**ieri/oggi/domani**
day/week/month/year	**giorno/settimana/mese/anno**
left/right	**sinistra/destra**
up/down	**su/giù**
good/bad	**buono/cattivo**
big/small	**grande/piccolo**
cheap/expensive	**buon mercato/caro**
hot/cold	**caldo/freddo**
open/closed	**aperto/chiuso**
free (vacant)/occupied	**liberto/occupato**
near/far	**vicino/lontano**
early/late	**presto/tardi**
right/wrong	**guisto/sbagliato**

Index

Numbers in **bold** refer to the main entry listed.